Indianapolis Union Station
Trains, Travelers, and Changing Times

A particular type of building causes particular emotional strings to resonate, and as long as that building stands, it will continue to play its own particular music in the human heart.

—Susan Neville
"Sacred Space in Ordinary Times"

Beautiful stained-glass wheel windows about twenty feet in diameter dominate the north and south walls of the head house, or central portion, of Indianapolis Union Station. (Photo by Darryl Jones)

INDIANAPOLIS UNION STATION

Trains, Travelers, and Changing Times

James R. Hetherington

Color photography by

Darryl Jones

Memorabilia provided by Richard K. Baldwin

Guild Press of Indiana, Inc.

Carmel, Indiana

GUILD PRESS OF INDIANA, INC.
435 Gradle Drive
Carmel, Indiana 46032
(317) 848-6421

ISBN 1-57869-079-0
Library of Congress Catalog Card Number 00-104416
Printed in China

Dustjacket photo by Darryl Jones

Dustjacket design by Listenberger Design Associates

Text design by Sheila G. Samson

The excerpted article appearing on page 83 of this book is reprinted by permission of AMERICAN HERITAGE Magazine, a division of Forbes, Inc., © Forbes, Inc.

The Pan American Plaza, just west of Union Station and in front of the Crowne Plaza Hotel, has become a popular place for visitors to downtown Indianapolis, particularly on a warm, sunny day. The plaza was part of the structures built for the Pan American Games held in Indianapolis in the late 1980s. (Photo by Darryl Jones)

To my wife, Susan,

    my helpmate of forty-seven years.

Her wise counsel and support make everything I do better.

A reminder of years gone by is this statue of a sailor waiting for his train. He is one of the "ghost people" created for the festival marketplace to add a touch of nostalgia to the station. Most of the ghost people are now located in the Crowne Plaza Hotel at Union Station. Our sailor is posed by the refurbished Pullman cars that now serve as luxury suites at the hotel. (Photo by Darryl Jones)

Union Station's clock tower was visible to much of the town in 1888, and many people set their timepieces by the station clock. The railroads introduced standard time in the United States, developing the four time zones in 1883. The clock towers reminded Americans that commerce moved to the tick of railroad time. (Photo by Darryl Jones)

Contents

Foreword

Railroads were probably the most important factor driving American economic growth in the last half of the nineteenth century. They brought the pork products of Cincinnati, the grain products of Indiana and Illinois, and the beef of the Great Plains to Eastern cities swelling with new immigrant populations. They shipped lumber and building supplies from the northern woods of Wisconsin to prairie cities such as Chicago and to the developing communities of the Great Plains. And railroads made possible inexpensive shipping of mass-produced consumer goods of the Eastern seaboard to the great inland section of America.

They moved people—millions of people! Midwestern merchants going East to examine and buy the pots and pans, bolts of cloth, and furniture that small-town people could now afford, along with immigrants coming to new homes and Easterners looking for a fresh start. And a new breed of travelers—middle-class vacationers exploring their country. Niagara Falls, reached after about ten train changes, was one of several mid-center vacation destinies.

To facilitate this great movement of goods and people, railroads built substantial facilities in the cities they served. While freight depots, grain elevators, and warehouses were built to service freight traffic, the truly wonderful railroad structures were the passenger stations. Rich in appearance and comfortable in their facilities, stations served both the needs of travelers and the needs their host cities had of presenting positive images of themselves.

And in this history of creating impressive passenger facilities, Indianapolis had a special role to play, for the nation's first union station was built here in 1853.

Jim Hetherington has done a wonderful job in writing this book and examining these themes. In it, he traces the growth of railroad service to and from Indianapolis, beginning in 1847 with the arrival of the Madison and Indianapolis Rail Road, continuing through the building of the country's first Union Depot in Indianapolis in 1853, and then tracing the long history of the current Union Station, built in 1886 and opened for traffic in 1888.

Describing the design and the building of the structure, Jim gives us a sense of its size and its purpose. He goes on to examine its initial renovation in the early years of the twentieth century, a time when steam railroads were facing serious competition from interurbans. He concludes the story by tracing the long, sad, gradual decline of the building that paralleled the decline of America's passenger train service.

But this is not a story solely of bricks and mortar. Jim devotes many engaging pages to the people who worked in or traveled through Indianapolis's two Union Stations. We read of a young telegraph operator named Thomas Edison; of ticket agents such as William "Uncle Billy" Jackson; of Ben Wesselman and Tom Smith, the current station's last railroad employees; and of children going away to school and war sweethearts, for whom the station was an important element in their lives.

For me, a non-Hoosier, perhaps the most fascinating part of this book is Hetherington's careful tracing of the growth of the city around the station. These include the development of surrounding streets and businesses, as well as the work that went into elevating the tracks in order to retain the easy connection between the north and south sides of town.

All in all, Jim Hetherington has performed an important service to those interested in urban history and railroad history. He has performed an even greater service for a community struggling with the issue of preserving Union Station, for he has reminded us how crucial railroads were to the development of Indianapolis, and how central Union Station remains to our sense of community.

Jerry Musich

Jerry Musich is a member of the advisory board of the Indiana Historical Society's Midwest Railroad Research Center. He is also a former executive director of the National Railroad Museum in Green Bay, Wisconsin, and is currently working on a book about Chicago's first railroad.

Introduction

When it opened in 1888, Union Station in Indianapolis was one of the culminating expressions, in brick and technology, of a city that had transformed itself in sixty years from a few cabins in a malarial swamp to an urban center justifiably calling itself "The Crossroads of America."

Over the years, Union Station has both reflected and effected changes in ever-changing Indianapolis. Indianapolis itself has depended on its transportation facilities, essential no matter what their form—whether as a dock for flatboats or an ultramodern airport. Any transportation center is an urban hub: a gathering place, a stimulus to commercial growth, a geographical and social center for the city, a colorful locale for the making of memories.

Thus it was in the beginning for Union Station. So it was in the years of its glory, 1890 to 1945. And so it is today, after years of decline and failed solutions—a hub of activity for the wheel that sends its spokes out from the circular center of one of the most important cities in the Midwest.

Almost from the time Indiana became a state in 1816, Governor Jonathan Jennings envisioned a new state capital in the center of the state, somewhere on White River. In 1820, with the approval of the state legislature, he appointed a ten-member commission to select a site for that new capital. The governor and his commission spent three days studying possible sites. After visiting the William Conner farm near Noblesville as well as a few other possible locations, they chose a site near the confluence of White River and Fall Creek.

Governor Jennings and his commission gave their selection careful thought, and history has proved their judgment sound. But, when they selected that site at White River and Fall Creek, they thought the river was navigable and that it would play a big part in the new capital's future. That was not the case. White River proved not to be navigable by anything but small boats. It took the railroad, which arrived in 1847, to put Indianapolis on the map.

After that first railroad, the Madison and Indianapolis Rail Road, reached Indianapolis, the city quickly became the center of a rail network that extended to every corner of the state. Then, it became an important cog in a rail system linking cities throughout the Midwest and across the nation, attracting commerce, industry, and people. Indianapolis became known locally and nationally as "The Railroad City."

The first union depot in America—"union" because it sought to serve all the railroads—was built here in 1853, attracting business developments and stimulating the growth of downtown. Today that area, known as the Wholesale District, is on the National Register of Historic Places.

The present Union Station was built in 1888 on the site of the original after the city had outgrown the old depot. The new station, too, quickly established its own important identity and became the gateway to Indianapolis for five decades of active service. Finally, after dying as an active depot for trains, Union Station today faces a sound future. In picture and words, this book chronicles the several lives of this familiar landmark.

A painter skillfully adds the finishing touches to the restoration work around one of the huge wheel windows in the head house. (Photo by Darryl Jones)

(*Above*) When all three stories of the old head house were renovated in the 1980s, the original beauty of the structure once again became apparent. Artistry worthy of Michaelangelo went into the restoration of the barrel-vaulted ceiling with its stained-glass skylights, lofting sixty-four feet above the station's terrazzo floor.

(*Left*) The ornate railings and light fixtures on the second- and third-floor balconies, along with the skylight, enhance the charm of the old station. (Photos by Darryl Jones)

chapter 1
From Pioneer Village to "The Railroad City"

In 1847, twenty-seven years after the first settlers moved to the area, Indianapolis was a town of about four thousand hardworking settlers. It had been the state capital since 1825, and despite many hardships—including a cholera epidemic, the state's financial Panic of 1837, and floods from White River—by the 1840s Indianapolis was beginning to prosper.

White River had not been deep enough to make Indianapolis a shipping center, but Indianapolis was connected to the rest of the country by one of the great pioneer highways in America—the National Road. Completed in the 1830s, the National Road brought thousands of migrants to the young city. Called Washington Street where it ran through town, it was then one hundred and twenty feet wide with a gravel bed in the center. The road was often filled with big, broad-wheeled Conestoga wagons loaded with merchandise or a family's possessions and drawn by six large horses. There were also people on foot, on horseback, in open wagons—most making their way to new homes in the West. A covered wooden toll bridge spanned White River.

Stores and taverns began to enjoy new prosperity, meeting the needs of the transients. Some of the travelers stayed to make a home in Indianapolis. By the 1840s the community reflected changing times. Necessities no longer had to be made at home or gone without. New businesses sprang up along Washington Street and along Maryland, Market, Pennsylvania, Meridian, and Illinois streets as well. Two pottery plants turned out decorative pieces as well as sets of "everyday" and fine dishes. Furniture stores offered well-made drop-leaf tables, corner cupboards, bedsteads, and trundle beds. Blacksmiths crafted fireplace andirons, plowshares, and garden hoes.

Lumberyards appeared on streets bordering the center of town, as virgin maple and walnut trees eighty feet high were felled to supply board for building. Culture and religion were not ignored: the Reverend Henry Ward Beecher, pastor of Second Presbyterian Church, began to attract national notice with his preaching and his writing; and the first amateur theater group, the Indianapolis Thespian Corps, was formed in 1840.

Despite the bustle of growing urban life, cattle still grazed in open fields just north of the first statehouse, which had been built in 1835 on the north side of Washington Street in front of where the present State Capitol stands.

And on the outskirts of town in the area beyond Tenth Street and east of Pogue's Run, the shadows of a forest still loomed.

Therefore, the arrival of the Madison and Indianapolis Rail Road in Indianapolis on October 1, 1847, was occasion for great celebration. Most

The area where the old Union Depot was built in 1853 is depicted in this drawing by Christian Schrader. Looking northwest from the corner of Pennsylvania and South streets, Pogue's Run passes between Smock and Nagley's Saw Mill and Morris Morris' Grist Mill. The grist mill, which burned down in 1851, was just east of Meridian Street. The asterisk at the left edge of the drawing is just west of Meridian Street and indicates where the depot was later built. The log cabin in the inset was on the site where the clock tower of the present Union Station now stands.

Schrader, who did his drawings from memory years later, wrote of this drawing: "Why I know this so well and why I drew this picture. It happened in the latter '40s and the early '50s when my father worked in the shops below South Street for the first railroad company in Indianapolis. It was then my duty as a boy to carry his dinners to him every day for several years. I crossed the creek on stepping stones." (Indiana State Library)

of the townsfolk had never seen a railroad or a locomotive before, and they could hardly comprehend speeds of twenty miles an hour, and they all turned out to see the first trains steam into town. Some even took an excursion to Franklin, Indiana, and back—children shouting in fear with cinders flying over the lawn dresses and frock coats of their parents.

Spalding's Circus was in Indianapolis that day, with the band of the celebrated bugler Ned Kendall, and the whole troupe, along with a company of cavalry, participated in a big parade to celebrate the arrival of the railroad. Governor James Whitcomb made a speech from the top of a railroad car, and afterward people headed "uptown" for the hotels on Washington and Meridian streets for dinner. That evening there were fireworks and "a general good time."

Historian W. R. Holloway, in *Indianapolis: A Historical and Statistical Sketch of the Railroad City* (1870), wrote:

> *With the opening of the Madison Railroad, there came with it such a change as comes upon boyhood at puberty. There was a change of features, of form, a suggestion of manhood, a trace of the beard, and voice of virility. Manufacturers appeared, and would not disappear. Stores that had formerly mixed up dry goods, groceries, grain, hardware, earthenware, and even books in their stock began to select and confine themselves to one or two classes of their former assortment. . . . The price of property advanced. A city form of government was adopted. A school system was inaugurated. Everybody felt the impulse, without exactly feeling its direction, of prosperity.*

In the three years after the arrival of the railroad, the population more than doubled, to 8,091. And by 1852, when work began on the town's—and the nation's—first Union Depot, Indianapolis had 10,800 inhabitants.

Those first trains to actually pull into Indianapolis that day in 1847 took a long time in getting there. In 1832, the state had chartered companies to build six railroads to center on Indianapolis. But no adequate means were provided for their construction and, in the condition of the country at that time, there would have been no profitable use for them.

At the time, the state was involved in a mammoth improvement program that included roads, canals, and railroads. The most costly project was the Central Canal, which was to link the Wabash and Erie Canal (running between Toledo, Ohio, and Lafayette) with the Ohio

Belle Fountain & Ind. Depot.

Cincinnati, Lawrenceburg & Ind. Depot.

Lafayette Depot.

Madison & Ind. Depot.

Four railroads built stations in Indianapolis prior to the opening of the Union Depot in 1853. The depots served lines for (*clockwise from the top left*) the Bellfountaine and Indianapolis; the Cincinnati, Lawrenceburg, and Indianapolis; the Madison and Indianapolis; and the Indianapolis and Lafayette railroads. (Indiana State Library)

River at Evansville. In 1836 the state had taken over several of the railroad companies and tried to save its faltering plan for a canal system by combining it with the railroads in a "great system" of railroads, canals, and turnpikes. Three years later, following the financial Panic of 1837, the state went bankrupt under the load, its finances broken by overzealous and impractical planning, terrible management, and corruption.

By that time the Madison and Indianapolis Rail Road had been completed from Madison, on the Ohio River, to Vernon, twenty miles to the north. The railroad was operated by the state's lessee, D. C. Branham & Company, until 1843, when the legislature authorized its sale. The new owner then proceeded to complete the road in increments—first to Scipio, then to Clifty Creek, on to Columbus, to Edinburg, to Greenwood, and finally—in October 1847—to Indianapolis.

In 1846, as the railroad approached Indianapolis, the company selected its depot ground on South Street, east of Pennsylvania. It was a quarter of a mile from the south edge of town, but the ground was high, cheap, and convenient. Soon the first angry complaints of citizens about the location died out in the excitement over the actual arrival of the railroad.

The depot would not go to the town, so the town went to the depot, building businesses all around it and creating for a time a separate commercial center there. Pogue's Run, which flowed between the town and the depot, was straightened from Virginia Avenue to Meridian Street by property owners, and the streets were graded and filled across the low, muddy space of the creek bottom.

The National Road had benefited Indianapolis, but the isolation of the town really ended with the completion of this railroad. The coming of the railroad indeed signified a revolution in the means of acquiring and disseminating goods. The long haul down the Mississippi River to New Orleans that Abraham Lincoln took as a young man was already an anachronism. Hogs and corn, which once took weeks to get to market in New Orleans, would now arrive at Eastern destinations within days. And travel time from East or South to the heartland was drastically shortened. A trip to Martin County from Lincoln, Massachusetts, by Indiana pioneer merchant Thomas Jefferson Brooks took four months in about 1820; three decades later, his sister made the same trip by rail (albeit with many stops and transfers) in a week.

Because the Madison line was the first to arrive, it could—and did—charge all that the traffic would bear. The high rates and heavy profits not only aroused opposition, but also spurred the development of competing lines. Within a very short time, eight railroads were completed, and Indianapolis became widely known as "the railroad city of the west."

By December 1848 no lines had as yet been finished to compete with the Madison, but several were under way or in the planning stage. The city fathers had decided that a common passenger depot was going to be a necessity. So, the council on December 20, 1848, authorized the creation of the Union Railway Company, which was to build a Union Depot and city tracks connecting the different railroads.

On December 19, 1849, four railroad companies adopted the following resolution:

> *Resolved, that it is expedient to locate and establish at Indianapolis a joint railroad track, connecting the Madison and Indianapolis, the Terre Haute and Richmond, the Peru and Indianapolis, and the Indianapolis and Bellfountaine railroads. And to locate and establish on said joint track a joint passenger depot for said companies.*

Later, the Peru railroad decided not to participate, so the other three companies became the founders of the Union Railway Company and the first Union Depot. Track construction was begun June 19, 1850, and, not long afterward, land was purchased for the depot, which was to be located on Louisiana Street between Meridian and Illinois streets, a short distance west of the Madison and Indianapolis depot. By 1852, the Indianapolis

Thomas Edison —
A Teenaged Inventor at Union Depot

When he was seventeen, Thomas A. Edison worked for a few months in 1864 at Indianapolis Union Depot as a telegraph operator for Western Union. Western Union ran most of the nation's railroad telegraph lines, and, by the mid-1860s, Indianapolis was a major rail shipping center and had earned the nickname "The Railroad City." Because the depot served as a junction for all the rail lines in the area, its telegraph office was busy and important.

Edison came here from Fort Wayne, where he had worked for a short time as a telegraph operator for the Pittsburgh, Fort Wayne, and Chicago Railroad. He got a job with Western Union as a plug (or novice) operator, working for seventy-five dollars a month.

Edison was assigned to the day shift on a "way wire," linking small towns. On the way wire, he could get by with a speed of ten to fifteen words a minute, but he aspired to the higher pay of an experienced operator. So, night after night, he returned to the office and sat by the man taking press dispatches for distribution to the city's newspapers.

At first, Edison couldn't distinguish the signals, much less copy down the messages. But he conceived the idea of using a repeating device that would record the incoming message on a paper tape and then play it back at a slower speed. Edison described his device this way:

> I got two old Morse registers and arranged them in such a way that by running a strip of paper through them, the dots and dashes were recorded on it by the first instrument as fast as they were delivered . . . and transferred to us through the other instrument at any desired rate of speed or slowness. They would come in at the rate of fifty words a minute and we would grind them out at the rate of twenty-five. Then weren't we proud. Our copy used to be so clean and beautiful that we hung it up on exhibition. The manager used to come and gaze at it in silence with a puzzled expression. . . . He could not understand it; nor could any of the other operators; for we used to drag off my impromptu automatic recorder and hide it when our toil was over.

As one of Edison's biographers wrote later, "It was a simple but clever device. It involved no great invention; yet it became the fountainhead of the most productive inventive career in the history of the world."

After leaving Indianapolis, Edison drifted from one job to another in the major cities of the Midwest and South. He went to work in Cincinnati in 1865. At every stop along the way, he spent his free time reading and experimenting.

Telegraphy focused his innate scientific curiosity and opened the door to much broader inquiries into electricity and electromagnetism.

and Bellfountaine; Indianapolis and Cincinnati; Jeffersonville and Indianapolis; Terre Haute and Richmond; Peru and Indianapolis; Indianapolis and Lafayette; and Indiana Central railroads were solidly under construction. The Union track, connecting all of these, had been completed. And the Union Depot was under construction.

"We were beginning to feel our importance as a railroad center," Holloway wrote, "and (we) exhibited our conceit in such sensible forms as new hotels, manufactures and business houses." Local historians seem to agree that no other city in the nation, maybe no other city in the world, had a union railroad depot at this time, making it of national significance when Indianapolis Union Depot opened on September 28, 1853.

By that time, the Union Railway Company was an association of five railroads, the original three plus the Indianapolis and Cincinnati and the Indiana Central. Other companies later occupied the depot as tenants. General T. A. Morris, as chief engineer, was in charge of the construction of the depot, and William N. Jackson was appointed as the first general ticket agent, secretary, and treasurer, jobs he held for many years.

Joseph Curzon, who had moved to Indianapolis in 1851 from Harrisburg, Pennsylvania, was named architect. A native of England, he was one of only six professional architects in Indianapolis in the 1850s, and he soon established a successful practice here. In addition to designing the Union Depot in 1852, he also was architect for such Civil War-era landmarks as Second Presbyterian Church, located at Pennsylvania and Vermont Streets, considered one of the most attractive buildings in the city at the time, and additions to the State Hospital for the Insane.

The first Union Depot was 120 feet wide and 420 feet long, with tracks inside for five passenger trains and two tracks for freight trains along the south side of the building. The brick-and-stone structure cost $30,000 to build. After the Union Depot opened, the Madison and Indianapolis Rail Road station was turned into a freight station.

In 1866 the depot was enlarged to two hundred feet wide and improved. An eating house was added, and the offices were transferred to the south side.

By 1870 the population of Indianapolis had grown to 48,244. The depot was handling an average of eighty trains a day, "many of them of great length." About two million passengers arrived or departed from the Union Depot that year. W. R. Holloway wrote, "The erection of a similar building and on a larger scale, now urgently demanded, must ere long become a necessity if the great convenience of one passenger depot for all our railway lines is to be continued."

(*Top*) The old Union Depot had five sets of tracks going in and out of the station. (Indiana Historical Society Bass Photo Co. Collection Neg. No. FOL 620) (*Below*) The arches over the tracks showed the names of the railroads that jointly owned and operated the station. (Indiana Historical Society Bass Photo Co. Collection Neg. No. 5881) If you look closely at the roof structure, you will see that each artist saw the station a little differently.

TO THE EAST!

Bee Line

VIA INDIANAPOLIS and CRESTLINE.

👉 **GOING EAST**

Trains leave INDIANAPOLIS.

No. 2,	No. 4,	No. 6,
2.05 A. M.	**10.00 A. M.**	**7.30 P. M.**

DAILY, EXCEPT SUNDAYS.

WAGNER'S, SANDERSON'S and GATES'

Palace Day & Sleeping Cars

Run on Train "No. 4" (see Time Table on 3d page)

FROM INDIANAPOLIS

To CLEVELAND, To BUFFALO,

To ROCHESTER { WITHOUT CHANGE!

And on Train "No. 6" (see Time Table on 3d page)

FROM INDIANAPOLIS

To BUFFALO, To ALBANY,

To NEW YORK CITY

Without Change

☞ Palace Car on Train "No. 4" connects at Rochester with **Wagner's Special Drawing Room Train**, which makes only four regular stops from Rochester, reaching New York at 7.00 P. M.

Get your Tickets to all points East, via Indianapolis and Crestline,

OVER THE RELIABLE **Bee Line**

For Sale at Union Depot, Indianapolis.

(31)

E. A. FORD, Gen'l Pass'r Ag't, Cleveland, O.

TO THE WEST!

INDIANAPOLIS AND St. LOUIS RAILWAY.

Via TERRE HAUTE, MATTOON and PANA.

👉 **GOING WEST**

Trains leave INDIANAPOLIS:

No. 3,	No. 5,	No. 1,
3.40 A. M.	**7.50 A. M.**	**7.35 P. M.**

DAILY, EXCEPT SUNDAYS.

ELEGANT COACHES

BY DAY, AND

PALACE SLEEPERS

BY NIGHT,

Run over the **Indianapolis & St. Louis Railway**, from Indianapolis, to Terre Haute, Mattoon, Pana, Alton and

To St. Louis { WITHOUT CHANGE!!

We run Three Express Trains Daily,

Through to St. Louis, where direct connection with each Train is made with Trains on the Missouri Pacific, South Pacific, North Missouri and Kansas Pacific R'ys, for all points in MISSOURI, KANSAS and COLORADO. See Time Table on last page.

☞ GET YOUR TICKETS to St. Louis, and all points West, Via Terre Haute, Mattoon and Pana, over the

Indianapolis & St. Louis R'y,

For Sale at Union Depot, Indianapolis.

S. F. PIERSON, Gen'l Ticket Ag't,

(31)

Bee Line, and I. & St. L. R. R., Cleveland & St. Louis.

In this timetable, dated January 2, 1871, the "reliable" Bee Line of the Cleveland, Columbus, Cincinnati and Indianapolis Railway and the Indianapolis and St. Louis Railway promoted passenger train service east and west out of Indianapolis. (From the collection of Richard K. Baldwin)

RAILROAD ADVERTISER.

Vol. 1, No. 1. Indianapolis, Ind., September 1, 1869. Price, 3 Cents.

THE Railroad Advertiser

will be enlarged, and published daily, on and after September 13th, 1869, and thoroughly distributed throughout all the business portions of the city, and all Railroad trains departing from this city, making it one of the best and cheapest means for the merchants and manufacturers of this city, to secure both Local and Transient trade.

R. R. City Printing Co.,
PRINTERS & PUBLISHERS,
Vinton's Block, opposite P. O.,
INDIANAPOLIS.
Publishers of The Western
Magazine for E____ MAY, 1881.

ISAAC DAVIS & CO.,

HATS,

M. A. Stowell

First Grand Prize,
THE
HIGHEST AWARD,

CORRECTED TO SEPTEMBER 3D, 1893.

"Look at the Map."

INDIANAPOLIS
TO THE
World's Fair
OVER THE
PENNSYLVANIA
SHORT LINE.

JOSEPH WOOD, E. A. FORD,
General Manager, Gen'l Passenger Agent,
PITTSBURGH, PA.

STEVENSON & FOSTER CO., PRINT, PITTSBURGH, PA.

I.B. and W.
Danville
ROUTE TO
CHICAGO
AND
THE NORTH
NORTH-WEST
C. and E.I. R'Y.

A. S. DUNHAM, W. H. PROUTY,
G. P. & T. Agt. Act. G. P. & T. Agt.
C. & E. I. R'y. I. B. & W. R'y.
Chicago, Ills. Indianapolis, Ind.

W. M. SHAW,
General Agent,
Cincinnati,
Ohio.

KANKAKEE LINE

TIME TABLES

CHICAGO
TO
Lafayette,
Indianapolis,
Louisville,
❖ Cincinnati

Through Tickets and Sleeping Car Berths can be secured at Ticket Offices
121 RANDOLPH STREET,
Near Corner Clark.
Depot foot of Lake St. and Depots foot of 22d and 39th Sts., Grand Pacific Hotel, Palmer House and Tremont House, Chicago; also, principal Ticket Offices in the Northwest.

M. E. INGALLS, C. W. BENDER,
President, Superintendent,
CINCINNATI, O. INDIANAPOLIS, IND.

WM. M. GREENE, JOHN EGAN,
General Manager, Gen'l Pass. and Ticket Agent,
CINCINNATI, O. CINCINNATI, O.

RAND, MCNALLY & CO., PRINTERS, CHICAGO.

chapter 2
A New Station at
"The Crossroads of America"

In the decade following the arrival of the railroad, the population of Indianapolis more than doubled. By 1860 Indianapolis had 18,611 residents and was the state's largest and most important city, surpassing both Madison and New Albany.

Evidence of the city's new prosperity was everywhere. Some men wore silk hats to work, and successful men earned as much as a thousand dollars a year. Stores such as Charles Mayer & Co. along Washington Street were busy and stayed open from 6:00 A.M. to 9:00 P.M. to catch the transient railroad trade. Travelers arriving in the city had a choice of more than a dozen hotels. And at night some homes and streets were lit by new gaslights.

The arming and supplying of portions of the Union Army, as well as transporting thousands of soldiers and traveling civilians during the Civil War, impelled significant growth and activity at Union Depot. As soon as the war was over and the economy was poised to grow, railroad expansion was a certainty.

In the early days, passenger cars had been crude, often with no more than wooden benches to sit on. But by the 1860s, trains had passenger cars with plush seats, wood paneling, water closets, gaslights, and heating stoves. They even had sleeping cars and parlor cars with lounge furniture. Passengers who could afford first-class accommodations could travel in style and comfort.

In Indiana, five railroad trunk lines crossed the state, running east and west. Three other systems went the length of the state, north and south. With about forty more small railroads in service by this time, most of

Indiana's cities and towns were served by rail. Indianapolis had become the center of this rail network—for freight as well as passenger business. It linked the state with Chicago, Cincinnati, Louisville, Pittsburgh, St. Louis, and other American cities across the continent. "The Railroad City" was now also being referred to as the "Crossroads of America."

But economic growth is never without its liabilities. For the railroads in the latter half of the nineteenth century, the competition was intense—at times, ruinous. Wild speculation in railroad stock, overbuilding, the endless rate wars for both passenger and freight business, and the economic crisis of 1873 led to widespread bankruptcy and complicated reorganization schemes. Although the railroads were often not financially successful, they stimulated the growth and economic prosperity of Indiana.

To connect all of the tracks entering the city, a belt railroad was built for the Union Stockyards in 1877. It was one of the first in America. In 1882 the Indianapolis Union Railway Company (as it was incorporated in 1872) leased the belt railroad for 999 years. The next year the Indianapolis Union Railway Company was reorganized in part for the purpose of seeking a new building. The need had existed for some time. Now, the five railroads owning an interest in the enterprise felt the time was right. The soot-stained, old depot simply could not handle the number of trains arriving and departing each day. Trains, and their passengers, frequently experienced long delays just waiting to get into the station.

James McCrea, general manager and later president of the Pennsylvania Railroad, was president of the Indianapolis Union Railway Company throughout the planning and construction of the new Union Station. He provided the vision and the leadership to get the station built. The Indianapolis Journal said in an article published in 1886:

> *The fact is that nothing would have been done for years to bring about a new union depot but for Mr. McCrea's persistent urging the matter. . . .* The Journal *has the best of authority for saying that the first time he met the board of directors, he brought the matter up, and there has not been a meeting since which he attended that the subject of a new union depot has not been discussed.*

Action became imperative in 1883 when the fifteenth railroad asked for accommodations on the union tracks and in the Union Depot. In December 1884 the directors of the company met and passed a resolution beginning the process. Also, V. T. Malott, vice president and general

James McCrea

James McCrea had the vision, persistence, and clout to get the new Indianapolis Union Station built. In recognition of his contribution, the two-block-long street just east of the station was named McCrea Street.

McCrea was promoted to manager of the Pennsylvania Railroad's southwest system, the lines west of Pittsburgh, in May 1882. Just prior to taking that position, he went on an inspection trip over some of the Pennsylvania lines with his predecessor, D. W. Caldwell. As the story goes, he had not been in the old Union Depot ten minutes when he remarked to his boss, Pennsylvania Railroad Vice President J. N. McCullough, "Well, the most needed improvement is a new union depot at Indianapolis." He also said that Meridian Street should be closed or a viaduct built over the tracks on that street before any new depot was built.

As manager of the Pennsylvania's lines that included Indianapolis, McCrea became a member of the board of directors of the Indianapolis Union Railway Company, and he immediately began pushing for the new station.

At McCrea's first board meeting, in May 1882, the board directed its president, William R. McKeen, to employ an architect to draft plans for a new Union Station. Months later, when the decision to build the new station was made, McKeen turned the presidency of the board over to McCrea, who retained that position until the building was completed.

In a story in *The Indianapolis Journal* on November 26, 1886, McCrea was praised as a friend of Indianapolis. The paper said "nothing would have been done for years to come about a new union depot but for

Railroad Museum of Pennsylvania, Pennsylvania Historical and Museum Commission

Mr. McCrea's persistent urging the matter." It also reported that the Pennsylvania Railroad had expended nearly $550,000 in other improvements in Indianapolis since McCrea took the managership in 1882.

As it turned out, the Meridian Street viaduct that McCrea sought was never built, primarily because of the demands of affected property owners. But James McCrea continued to do the job for the Pennsylvania Railroad. He also continued to receive promotions, and on January 2, 1907, he was elected president of the Pennsylvania system. On October 27, 1907, McCrea participated in the opening of a Union Station in Washington, D.C., and in 1910, he presided over the completion of the railroad tunnel under the Hudson River into New York City and the opening of New York's Penn Station. This was the high point of his career. When McCrea died in 1913, he left a legacy as a builder for his railroad and the communities it served.

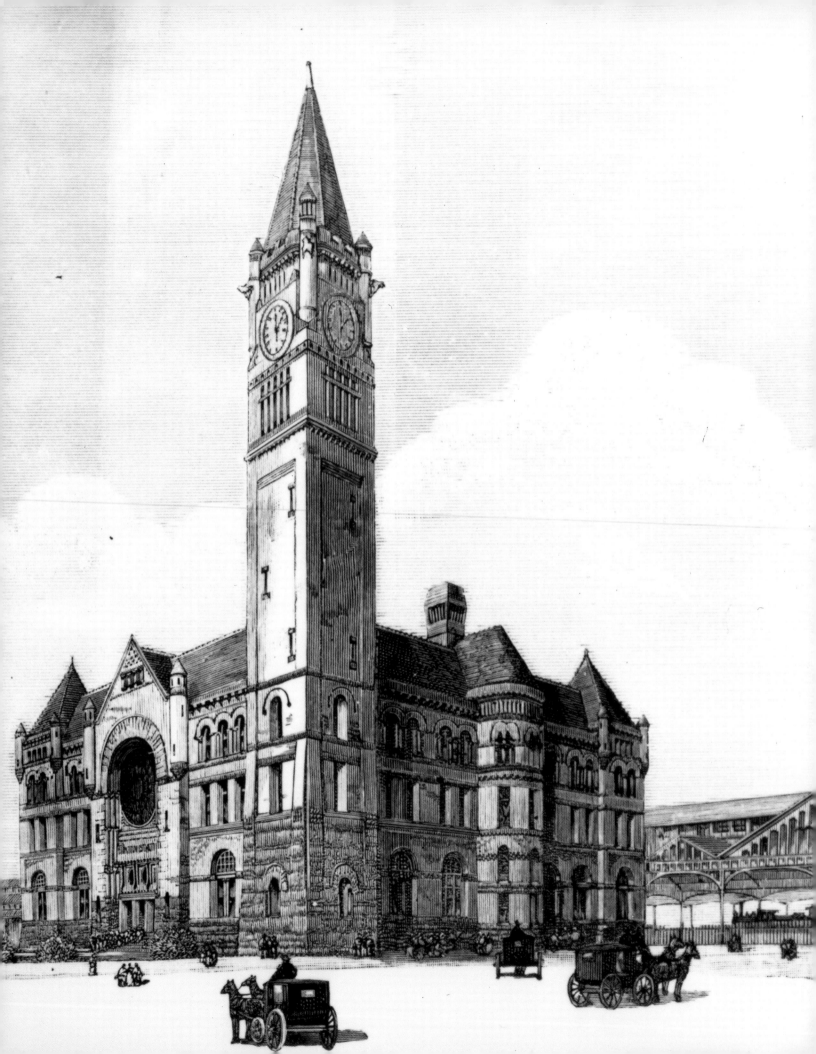

manager of the Indianapolis Union Railway Company, was instructed to push through the state legislature "such legislation as was needed in the way of vacating streets and providing for other necessaries."

Thomas Rodd, an architect and engineer from Pittsburgh, was hired to design the new Union Station. F. C. Doran, of Richmond, Indiana, assisted him. The drawings they produced called for a three-story structure of red brick and granite with extensive use of Romanesque arches in the design. A 185-foot clock tower was the dominant feature.

Legislative approval came in March 1885, and options on the needed real estate were immediately sought. At the same time, *The Journal* reported, "legislation was being pushed through the City Council and Board of Aldermen, this work being rather tedious."

By September 1886, James McCrea was able to report that "the city authorities have acted very honorably with the company, in fact granting them all the favors they expected, and the Union Railway Company now has good titles to every piece of property between Illinois and Meridian streets, both north and south of the Union Depot, which they need, with one exception, and the property is paid for."

As part of its agreement with the city, the railway company was to make improvements to the Illinois Street tunnel, construct a viaduct over Meridian Street, and cover part of Pogue's Run, over which tracks were to be laid. The tunnel had been built in 1872 for the use of the mule-drawn trolleys. Pogue's Run, a meandering creek flowing from the east side past Woodruff Place and the Civil War Arsenal, passed just north of the depot. Flooding frequently, it had been a problem since the first Union Depot was built.

In November 1886, Joseph Downey of Chicago was awarded the contract for construction of the station proper, including everything except the electric lighting. C. J. Shultz of Pittsburgh received the contract to build the train sheds. Before the end of the year, hundreds of carloads of stone had been hauled in for construction of the station's foundation, and the excavation work had begun.

The new Union Station was built between Illinois and Meridian streets just north of the existing station, which remained in use during much of the construction of the new facility. The old station was torn down in the summer of 1888 to allow completion of the new train sheds. By that time, the general ticket agent and his staff were able to move to temporary quarters in what was to be a baggage room when the new station was completed. Other occupants of the old depot moved to nearby buildings.

An artist's rendering, probably done while the building was under construction, shows how the new Union Station was to look when it was completed. (Indiana Historical Society Bass Photo Co. Collection Neg. No. FOL 619)

Thomas Rodd

Thomas Rodd, an architect and engineer from Pittsburgh, designed the new Union Station and supervised its construction. It seems it was by more than chance that he got the job—for, at the time, Rodd was an employee of the Pennsylvania Railroad.

Rodd was born in London, England, in 1849, a few years before his family emigrated to the United States. At the age of thirteen, he entered the U.S. Navy and served until the end of the Civil War, when he entered the U.S. Naval Academy.

Rodd resigned from the Naval Academy prior to his last exam in 1869, when he found that graduation would involve an extended cruise that would delay his pursuing an engineering career. Three years later, he went to work for the Pennsylvania Railroad.

While employed by the Pennsylvania system, Rodd built a large and lucrative private practice as a civil engineer, which was considered very unusual for a person with such a position with a large system of railroads. It was as a private practitioner that he was hired by the Indianapolis Union Railway Company to design and build its new passenger station.

The fact that Rodd lived in Pittsburgh may also have influenced his design for Union Station, since the Romanesque-style Allegheny County courthouse, in Pittsburgh, was built about the time Rodd was working on his plans for the station. The Allegheny County courthouse was the work of architect Henry Hobson Richardson, the man generally credited with popularizing Romanesque architecture in America.

Shortly after he finished Union Station, Rodd was involved in rebuilding the Pennsylvania Railroad facilities destroyed by the Johnstown flood. Between 1895 and 1901, he designed and directed the construction of works valued at more than $10 million, including Westinghouse facilities in East Pittsburgh and Manchester, England, and Union Switch and Signal Company works at Swissvale, Pennsylvania.

In 1899 the Pennsylvania Railroad promoted Rodd to chief engineer of the lines west of Pittsburgh, a position he held for twenty years.

Today, Indianapolis Union Station is still regarded by some experts as an outstanding example of Romanesque Revival architecture, with its extensive use of the Roman arch in its design and its predominant exterior materials: red pressed brick over an exposed foundation of rock-faced red granite. The variation in detail floor by floor is also typical, as are the upper-story tourelles with conical caps, the continuous hood moldings of round arches, and the use of medieval motifs of decoration, such as the entwining foliar patterns.

Union Station is one of the oldest examples of Romanesque Revival architecture in the state. It is also the largest and most impressive example of a nineteenth century railroad station in Indiana. In 1974 it was added to the National Register of Historic Places.

By June 1888 the tunnel improvements had been completed, and the trolleys were not the only ones to benefit. *The Indianapolis Journal* reported that "the Illinois Street tunnel under the Union tracks is daily becoming more popular (with the public) as a driveway. It is now so light and airy that it is much preferred to waiting for trains at the grade crossings."

Not long afterward, heavy iron girders were placed over Pogue's Run between Meridian and Delaware Streets and tracks were laid over them, "greatly increasing the facilities at the east end of the station." But the viaduct to carry Meridian Street traffic over the grade-level tracks was not to be. The city wanted it, and the railroads were willing to pay a reasonable price for it, but it had become a source of great controversy. There were arguments over the width and exact location of the viaduct. Property owners, whose property might be taken or businesses hurt by construction of the new railroad bridge, filed lawsuits.

Even after the new station opened, the executive committee of the

Until the tracks through Union Station were elevated following World War I, this tunnel under the Illinois Street tracks was used by trolleys and others who sought to avoid the delays caused by trains at the grade-level crossings. Once the tracks were elevated, the tunnel was eliminated in 1919. (Indiana State Library)

railroad was empowered to proceed with the work as soon as the question of damages was settled, so that the company could know where it stood in the matter. But, ultimately, Meridian Street was left, in the words of *The Journal*, "as it has been for thirty years, a very dangerous and inconvenient crossing of the Union tracks."

The old Union Depot had been electrified in 1882, and when the new facility was built the station and train sheds were illuminated with sixty-five arc lights and 1,150 incandescent lights provided by the Indianapolis Jenney Electric Light Company. Power was generated by four stationary engines in the basement of the station, and the building was heated with natural gas.

Early in 1888 the railroad board announced that the dining rooms in the new station would go "not to the man who will pay the most for the lease, but to the party who will give the best table service." In June Thomas Taggart of Indianapolis was selected as the best man to take charge of the depot restaurant.

Taggart, an amiable Irishman active in Democratic politics in Indianapolis, had worked in railroad restaurants since he was fifteen years old. He came to Indianapolis in 1877 to work in the restaurant at the old depot. He became sole proprietor of the restaurant in the new station,

President Benjamin Harrison, shown here with his family going to his inauguration, was elected President in 1888, the year Union Station was built. The station played an important role in Harrison's campaign since he chose not to travel, conducting instead a "front-porch" campaign. Representatives of the national press, political delegations, and celebrities came to Indianapolis to see him in such numbers they significantly boosted passenger travel through Union Station. (President Benjamin Harrison Home)

later acquiring control of the Grand Hotel and the Denison Hotel in Indianapolis and the French Lick Hotel in French Lick, Indiana. He is best remembered, however, as one of the city's most powerful politicians, serving as mayor from 1895 to 1901. He sat on the Democratic National Committee for sixteen years, serving as chairman from 1904 to 1908.

One of the last, and most prominent, features of the new station to be put in place was the giant clock that was to enhance the station's distinctive tower and be visible for a great distance in all directions. Fredrick Herron of Indianapolis received the contract to provide the clock, which was to have four dials, each nine feet in diameter, and was to be lighted at night by electricity.

Diners in Taggart's Union Station Dining Room were offered many delectable selections. This menu from November 22, 1888, features a variety from down-home short ribs of beef with brown potatoes to elegant lobster salad. Travelers could relax with their meal without fear of missing their trains, as the restaurant held the policy that "Departure of all trains will be duly announced." (Program Collection, Indiana State Library)

The *General*, a famous locomotive built in the 1850s and stolen from Southern forces during the Civil War, was restored in the 1960s by the Louisville and Nashville Railroad for its anniversary and was used for tours. In 1963 the restored steam engine was parked for a while on the original main line of the Big Four to Chicago, which was on the tow path of the downtown canal. The Indiana State Capitol can be seen in the background. (Photo by Richard K. Baldwin)

chapter 3
The Station Opens to Rave Reviews

On Sunday, September 16, 1888, the Indianapolis Union Railway Company began moving into its permanent quarters in the new building, which was to be called Union Station, replacing the old Union Depot. *The Indianapolis Journal*, which regularly carried the most railroad news of the three Indianapolis newspapers, published a lengthy story that day describing the new station:

> *The station proper is 150 feet square, three stories high, with basement and attic rooms. The tower is 185 feet high, and besides this structure there are two baggage rooms, one at the west and the other at the east end of the train sheds. The baggage rooms are each 150 feet long by twenty-five feet wide.*
>
> *The train sheds are 741 feet long by 200 feet wide, constructed of iron with a tin roof. The station proper rests on a granite foundation, the stone coming from Iron Mountain, Missouri. The walls above are constructed of pressed brick, with brown-stone trimmings, which were shipped from Pennsylvania. . . . Under cover of the sheds are ten long tracks, 741 feet long, and two short tracks. . . .*

The article went on to say that, after entering the main entrance and vestibule, "one comes to the gentlemen's waiting-room, 144 feet long by fifty feet wide." The sixty-five-foot-high ceiling of the room was a semicircle. On the west side was the package room, then the Union news room, next the barber's shop, and in the center—"one of the most elegant and complete ticket offices in this country."

The "official portrait" of the newly completed Union Station. It was taken at the request of the architect, Thomas Rodd, by J. W. Taylor of Chicago. (Indiana Historical Society Bass Photo Co. Collection Neg. No. FOL 620)

Directly adjoining the ticket office is the ladies' sitting and elegant private room. The ladies' room is seventy feet long by forty feet wide and finished in an attractive manner, one feature being a huge fireplace constructed of red sandstone shipped from Wisconsin.

Crossing to the east side of the main waiting room comes the dining room, which is sixty feet long by forty feet wide. Next to that is the sleeping-car office, which faces the general ticket office, the serving room for the dining rooms being in the rear. Adjoining this is the lunch counter.

The rooms on the first floor were twenty-two feet high, elaborately finished in native oak and brass. The second floor could be reached by an elevator or by stairways at either end of the main waiting room, which led to second and third floors containing eight large rooms each sixty feet long by twenty wide, and four each thirty feet long by twenty wide. Those on the second and third stories were supposed to be occupied by the Western Union Telegraph Company and superintendents of the different railroads. Cathedral and plate glass enhanced the light and beauty of the entire building, and the floors were constructed of tile "tastily arranged."

The newspaper also reported:

The Indianapolis Union Railway Company has thus far expended $1,156,000, part of which was for the Pogue's Run improvement, the tunnel on South Illinois Street, the asphalt and concrete pavements about the building and the streets around the building. There is still considerable to do in the way of putting on the finishing touches, which will increase the cost of the improvement to $1,200,000.

Some passenger trains had begun using the new train sheds a couple weeks earlier, and on Monday, September 17, travelers were able to see and use the new station as well. Although the grand opening was another exciting day for Indianapolis, it went unmarked by the parades, speeches, and fireworks of the occasion when the first trains arrived in 1847. Thousands of persons turned out to see the new facilities, however, all seeming to agree it was probably "the finest" union station anywhere. But there was no special ceremony. Of the three daily newspapers, only *The Indianapolis News* reported the story on page one. *The News*'s story on Monday began:

Yesterday was a busy day at the new Union Passenger Station. The building had been declared ready for occupancy, and a large force was busily engaged in moving the furniture and all appurtenances into it from the temporary quarters, where they have been established for several months. At midnight last night the task was complete. The great structure was brilliant with electric lights, the engines in the basement moved off in perfect order furnishing both light and heat. The employees appeared in blue uniforms and white caps, and like a transformation scene on the stage, everything was changed entirely. This morning the rush to the State Fair began, and the crowds found everything ready to accommodate them. Travelers of broad experience declare the Indianapolis passenger station to be the finest in the United States. In this connection it is well to remember that the old Union Station, lately demolished to make way for the new, was the first union depot in the country, and at the time of its erection in 1853, was much the finest structure of the kind in existence. Thus it is that Indianapolis is always in the van of progress.

The Indianapolis Sentinel reported:

Ticket-agent [Daniel] Donough is much pleased with his quarters. "It is absolutely," he says, "the finest ticket office in the United States." Tom Taggart's lunchrooms are open this morning, fully prepared for the multitude who are already coming for the fair. The rooms on the upper floors, with the exception of the telegraph room, are not ready for occupancy.

On Tuesday, *The Journal* reported: "Louis Reibold, the proprietor of the Bates House, who has traveled extensively in this and foreign countries, says that, taken as a whole, it is the finest and most complete structure he has seen, the beauty of it being that it is original with the architect, no idea having been borrowed from any railway station built prior to this one."

At the time of the grand opening, the major complaint was that the viaduct over Meridian Street had not been built. There were minor complaints as well. The express companies weren't too happy about being relegated for the most part to offices across the street. At the time, there were 6 express companies, employing locally about 130 men and requiring, as *The Railroad Gazette* reported, "four two-horse wagons and 24 single wagons to do the delivering, calling and depot work."

Union Station, shown here as it looked shortly after it was completed in 1888, is considered a fine example of Romanesque Revival architecture. The early Romans developed the dome and the arch to create stone bridges and open, airy public buildings. Historians commonly refer to these important engineering developments as Romanesque. During the Middle Ages, builders turned to Roman architecture, using the dome and arch to construct cathedrals and castles. Nineteenth-century architects again looked for inspiration in the classic forms, reviving the medieval Romanesque designs and building depots and other buildings in a style we now call Romanesque Revival. (Indiana Historical Society Bass Photo Co. Collection Neg. No. 824)

On September 22, *The Indianapolis Journal* reported another complaint:

> There is a good deal of complaint among the male population who are not admitted to the ladies' [waiting] room in the new Union Station. This is a rule at all large railway stations in this country and will doubtless be enforced until men have better habits. There should be one room at a large railway station, in fact, at a small one as well, where a lady can move about without her skirts dragging in tobacco spit.

(*Above*) This turn-of-the-century postcard shows a view of Illinois Street looking south toward the Spencer House, a popular stop for Union Station travelers.

(*Right*) A locomotive emerges from the train shed in this postcard scene from about 1912.

New Station for a "New" City

When Union Station opened in the fall of 1888, it became part of a "new" Indianapolis, a city just entering the age of electricity, telephones, inside plumbing, paved streets, and modern brick and stone buildings.

Indianapolis Brush Electric Light and Power Company, a predecessor of Indianapolis Power and Light Company, was founded in 1881, with the company using the old Union Depot for its first display of arc lighting. On January 11, 1882, the first electric lights clicked on in the depot. People from miles around turned out to watch the newfangled bulbs glow. The first incandescent lighting of a private home in Indianapolis occurred in 1889. At first the city fathers had little faith in electric lights, but by 1897 more than 800 electric lights glowed on Indianapolis streets, marking the end of the gaslight era.

Indianapolis residents saw Alexander Graham Bell's new wonder at the State Fair in 1877, and in 1879 the state's first telephone exchange was established in Indianapolis. Long distance was introduced in 1893, and by 1895 the Central Union Telephone Company had more than two thousand subscribers.

In the 1880s the Indianapolis Water Company, successor to the Water Works Company, began laying water mains and sewers throughout the city. Most homes still had backyard "privies," but more and more were featuring the new "water closets." Pumps were still a front and backyard fixture, but these, too, were being moved indoors, and the new faucets were being installed in the more expensive homes.

A major improvement in the city's mule-drawn streetcar system came in 1890, when the first electric streetcars were put into operation shortly after they had been pioneered elsewhere. Introduced along the Illinois Street line, amid large crowds of fascinated spectators, the electric streetcars replaced their mule-drawn predecessors almost instantly. By 1894 electrification of the city system was complete and the mules had been turned out to pasture.

In 1876 the new Marion County Courthouse was completed on Washington Street. Soon after, on the northwest side of the Circle, curving gracefully with its wide arc, were two more handsome, new buildings, the English Opera House and the English Hotel. The opera house opened September 27, 1880, and the English Hotel in 1884. A second section of the hotel was built in 1896.

In 1886 Tomlinson Hall, on Market Street, was dedicated as the new site for conventions, political rallies, lectures, balls, and the annual Flower Mission Fair. The hall, with its forty-two-hundred-seat capacity, resulted from a bequest from the estate of public-spirited druggist Stephen D. Tomlinson. The hall site also became a marketing center for the city's housewives as the ground floor of Tomlinson Hall housed an extensive fresh vegetable market, and the new City Market adjoined it on the east. The City Market was built in 1886 on the site originally designated in the 1821 plat of the city.

Only a few days after Union Station opened in September 1888, the new Indiana State Capitol Building was completed at its present site at Capitol Avenue and Washington Street. The huge Indiana limestone structure with its copper-covered dome cost nearly two million dollars to build—almost twice as much as Union Station.

In the 1880s and 1890s downtown streets were paved with bricks and cedar blocks. The Circle, so long neglected and scraggly, was neatly landscaped, its grass and gravel walks dominated by a statue of Oliver P. Morton, the Civil War governor.

Nearby were the fashionable streets—Meridian, Pennsylvania, and Delaware—where the wealthy and prominent families lived in mansions set back from the street behind iron fences and well-trimmed lawns. There were eighteen churches in the downtown area. And Indianapolis was becoming known for its fine hotels and restaurants, including the prestigious, 250-room Denison Hotel, built in 1880 at Ohio and Pennsylvania Streets.

Also in the 1880s, bicycles became a popular form of transportation and recreation. Young men took their best girls riding on the new tandem bikes, the bicycle built for two. In the 1890s the first automobiles appeared on Indianapolis streets.

Sports began to occupy Indianapolis residents' time and interest. Just about everyone played croquet, and baseball became a favorite pastime. Indianapolis fielded organized baseball teams as early as 1867, and from 1887 to 1890 the Hoosier capital had a major league team. In 1901 Indianapolis became a charter member of the American Association. Golf debuted in the 1890s, and Indiana's first bona-fide golf course, the Indianapolis Country Club, was built in 1897 on the site of the present Woodstock Club.

By 1890 Indianapolis was twice the size of Evansville, the state's second largest city. Seventy years after its founding, Indianapolis had 105,436 inhabitants. To boost this "modern" city was a new Commercial Club, predecessor of today's Chamber of Commerce, founded in 1890 by William Fortune, a newspaperman, and Colonel Eli Lilly, the pharmaceutical manufacturer and the club's first president.

By 1895 Indianapolis had a growing school system with forty-five grade schools and two high schools. The first high school, Indianapolis High School, was renamed Shortridge High School in 1897 in tribute to longtime superintendent Abram C. Shortridge. The second high school, Industrial Training High School, was later renamed Emmerich Manual Training High School in honor of its first principal, Charles Emmerich.

Years later, some old-timers looking back on Indianapolis in the 1880s and 1890s described that period as "the golden years." Union Station is a surviving part of that era.

Downtown Indianapolis around Union Station was a busy place at the turn of the century. (Indiana Historical Society Bass Photo Co. Collection Neg. Nos. C553 *[left]* and 16392 *[right]*)

William N. Jackson

The open square just north of Union Station is known as Jackson Place in honor, not of the nation's seventh president, but rather of William N. Jackson, affectionately known to many residents of nineteenth-century Indianapolis as "Uncle Billy."

Jackson was the first general ticket agent at the old Union Depot and the first secretary and treasurer of the Union Railway Company. He had strong managerial skills and great sensitivity to the needs of the traveling public, and over a period of many years, he was instrumental in making the Union Depot, and later Union Station, as hospitable as possible.

According to his obituary in *The Indianapolis News*, "He never married. He never held public office nor was identified with public affairs, and yet no man in his community and few men in any community have been wider known or more universally loved." Jackson was a man of deep religious convictions who shunned personal wealth, gave generously to charity, and urged the legislature to pay off some of the state's debt at a time when that was an unpopular position to take.

He was born in 1809 in Elk Forge, Maryland, and first came to Indianapolis in 1834 to close a small, unsuccessful iron business he and a brother had founded. He later worked in Terre Haute before returning to Indianapolis. He was an early member of Second Presbyterian Church, where Henry Ward Beecher was pastor from 1839 to 1849, remaining a member of that church until his death in 1900.

At the time of Jackson's death, *The Indianapolis News* published an interview with a longtime friend, Thomas H. Spann, who said Jackson "no doubt was more instrumental in building railroads in Indiana than any other man." In 1840, after seeing one of the early railroads in the east, Jackson persuaded a group of investors to build a railroad from Madison to Indianapolis, rather than the macadamized road they had planned to build. He was connected with the Madison and Indianapolis Rail Road (later the Jeffersonville,

Madison and Indianapolis Railroad) from 1844 until 1853. In July 1853 he met a friend who offered him the position of ticket agent, secretary and treasurer at the then new Union Depot.

Later, at the request of the directors of the J. M. & I. Railroad, Jackson returned reluctantly to Madison to take charge of the railroad and get it out of deep financial trouble. There was no money in the treasury, but Jackson succeeded in persuading all the creditors to withdraw their claims, based on his promise that he would use all the income to pay the workers and other operating expenses, and afterward the debts, as far as possible. He gradually got the trains running regularly again and succeeded in paying off many of the debts in the next two or three years.

When Jackson returned to Indianapolis in 1857 he was given back his job at Union Depot. He held all three positions until 1874, when he resigned as general ticket agent. In 1889 he gave up his responsibilities as treasurer of the Indianapolis Union Railway Company, but he was still secretary of the company when he died at the age of ninety-one. "Despite his age," *The News* reported, "Mr. Jackson seldom failed to be at his office at least part of each day, as he was possessed of not only marvelous vitality, but a strong will as well."

chapter 4
"A Proper Gateway to the City"

The decade following the opening of Union Station brought phenominal growth in railroad services. By 1900, about 150 passenger trains were arriving and departing each day from Indianapolis Union Station. One of the nation's finest trains, the Big Four's *Southwestern Limited*, provided all-Pullman service between St. Louis, Indianapolis, Cleveland, and New York. The New York Express, on the Pennsylvania Lines, sped passengers from St. Louis and Indianapolis to Columbus, Ohio, Pittsburgh, and the east. The Monon Line's *Indianapolis Special* served passengers bound for Chicago and points west, rumbling north out of town past growing suburbs clustered around Thirty-eighth Street and out to Broad Ripple.

At the time, in fact, several railroad lines had an *Indianapolis Special.* Indeed, Indianapolis was special. As the world turned into the twentieth century, few cities in America had a large and beautiful passenger station to accommodate all of their train-riding public. Few cities were served by as many as fifteen railroads, or by a belt railroad circling much of the city to conduct switching and transfer operations for all its railroads. And few had as many as 150 passenger trains arriving and departing each day.

Indianapolis had all of these. It was still Railroad City. And city and railroad officials from other parts of the country came here regularly to see how it functioned. But the tremendous growth of rail travel—and of the population—posed problems as well as opportunities for Indianapolis and the railroads that served it.

Within a very few years of the time the new Union Station opened, it was being called inadequate, and there were demands for expansion. In 1902 *The Journal Handbook of Indianapolis* said those who planned and built the new station "did not dream of the rapid growth of Indianapolis

Automobile use became increasingly common after World War I, and the elevation of the railroad tracks resulted in more traffic around Union Station and the surrounding business district. Convenient parking along Illinois Street became available once the tunnel was eliminated, as seen in this photo from August 25, 1922. One of the head house wheel windows looks north over part of Jackson Place, named after William N. Jackson. (Indiana Historical Society Bass Photo Co. Collection Neg. No. 79525F)

that was just then fairly starting on its new era of prosperity, and now it is seen that a building of almost twice the size of the present one is as badly needed as a new and larger one was in 1887." In fairness, it would have been difficult for anyone to anticipate the growth of the city. The population of Indianapolis more than doubled in the twenty years from 1880 to 1900, and it nearly doubled again in the next twenty years as it reached 314,194 persons in 1920.

To add to the problems of growth at the existing facilities, the dangers and delays for street traffic led to new demands for a Meridian Street viaduct. Wherever the ever-widening thoroughfares crossed the railroad tracks, there were major problems. The tracks simply had to be raised. In 1894 the Commercial Club had established a commission to work in a public way with municipal authorities to promote the elevation of the tracks. The commission was headed first by Colonel Eli Lilly, then by William Fortune, who became a key figure in the effort for elevation.

The railroads resisted the formidable costs of elevation, which by 1899 were estimated at $9 million for an earth embankment and $19 million for a steel trestle. The community was divided over the issue as well. It took several years, too many accidents, and legislative action by the Indiana General Assembly before much happened.

A fire at Union Station in the early years of the century drew lots of attention and lots of fire-fighting equipment, but the blaze caused only minor damage. (Indiana Historical Society Bass Photo Co. Collection Neg. No. FOL 620)

Clearly, the tracks were a hazard to citizens, with sixty-nine grade-level crossings in the city, many of them in the downtown area. Mothers carrying babies or holding children by the hand had to cross on foot. Horse carriages sometimes stopped on the tracks. The first automobiles bumped over as best they could. In wet weather, Pogue's Run flowed over the tracks at some points.

For many years, residents on Indianapolis's south side felt as if they were second-class citizens, not receiving all the city services or the appreciation accorded residents in other parts of the city. The railroad tracks, they complained, seemed to divide the city. Southsiders were among the most vocal advocates for the elevation of the tracks through the central part of the city. One might say they felt they were "on the wrong side of the tracks." Still, a decade passed with nothing done.

In a series of newspaper articles on the issue in 1914, one prominent citizen, William D. Woods, likened the Indianapolis Union Railway tracks to the Mason-Dixon Line. Retiring Mayor Harry Wallace, who lived on the south side, told southsiders they were not being discriminated against "on every occasion." He said, "With the elevation of the railroad tracks now under way, and which to my mind is the greatest need of the South Side, the so-called dividing line will be a thing of the past."

But not everyone agreed with the plans for the track elevation. While some wanted the tracks elevated so the street levels would remain the same, others wanted the streets depressed so that the tracks could still serve existing freight houses and railroad sidings. Some wanted the railroads to move their freight houses to the outskirts of the city, a plan to which downtown shippers objected. The Board of Trade in Indianapolis formed a strong partnership with the railroads to oppose the elevation. It took time to work out compromises and resolve all the issues.

In 1913 a committee of the Track Elevation Commission concluded its report with this statement:

It is now nearly twenty years since the elevation of tracks was first seriously proposed for the city, and some progress has been made, mainly on the outskirts of the city, but the main work as first laid out has hardly been touched as yet, only the approach from the west having been completed. The main streets are still open to the same dangers and complaints of the days of the first railroads, increased and intensified by the vast increase in traffic and in required speed of travel both on railroads and streets. The committee therefore wishes to emphasize to the utmost the need for promptness in getting action and

(*Left*) Trains moving out of the station heading east before the tracks were elevated often held up street traffic regularly, but, with the tracks at street level, passengers could leave the trains when they stopped and visit nearby shops and restaurants. (Indiana Historical Society Bass Photo Co. Collection Neg. No. 224829F)

(*Below*) Wagons, cars and pedestrians on Meridian Street stream across the tracks after waiting for a train to move off the crossing. Repeated efforts to get the agreements necessary to build a viaduct over the tracks on Meridian Street failed, and, according to *The Indianapolis Journal*, this crossing was "a very dangerous place" until the tracks were elevated after World War I. (Indiana Historical Society Bass Photo Co. Collection Neg. No. FOL 620)

Before the construction of the new train shed, passengers often had to walk across the tracks to board their trains. (Indiana Historical Society Bass Photo Co. Collection Neg. No. 70410F)

is willing to concede some details if thereby the time of completing the elevation of the east and west tracks through the heart of the city can be shortened.

In that same report, the committee called for enlarging and improving the station and making it "a proper gateway to the city." The committee said, "The Union Station in the modern city is its gateway and is the first structure by which the traveler can judge the beauty and dignity of the city." Having one passenger station to serve all railroads "gives an opportunity to make the structure one commensurate in dignity and beauty as well as in size and completeness of equipment with its importance as the only entrance to the city and the receiving point of the millions of visitors and new arrivals landing in the city, not to mention the other millions who spend but a few minutes about the station as they pass through."

Some track elevation projects over specific streets, mostly in outlying areas, began to occur as early as 1905, when tracks were elevated at Tenth Street and Massachusetts Avenue, and in 1906, when work was started on elevations over Kentucky Avenue and Missouri Street. But 1913 was really the beginning of a decade of modernization affecting Union Station and the wholesale district surrounding it.

Early in January 1913, the Indianapolis Union Railway Company authorized the expenditure of $120,000 for the immediate remodeling of Union Station. This work did not involve the elevation of the tracks through the station, but it did expand the capacity of the station and give the interior an entirely new appearance.

In its 1913 year-end review edition, *The Indianapolis Star* reported that the changes at Union Station increased the capacity of the building "fully 50 percent." It said the space on the first floor occupied by the women's waiting room and the lunchroom had been converted into a general lobby connecting with the former center lobby, making a large t-shaped room. Stairways were changed, an elevator installed, and two additional doors provided at the main entrance to the concourse. *The Star* went on to report:

> *An attractive marquise, 17 feet wide and 48 feet long, has been erected at the main entrance at Jackson Place. Another important feature of the remodeling plan was the installation of an immigrants' waiting room in the southwest corner of the basement. Entrance to this room is by means of an outside stairway. The remaining portion of the west section of the basement has been converted into a woman's cozy rest room.*
>
> *In the northeast section of the basement is the barber shop, with lavatories and smoking rooms. Baths have been provided in connection with the barber shop.*
>
> *The change in the upper floors, aside from extensive redecorating, has not been extended to the north. An attractive feature of the improvement is the new lighting arrangement. Around the balcony are a number of ornamental lamp posts similar in design to those used in the downtown streets, each holding three powerful lamps.*
>
> *To obtain better light by day, the art glass windows at the north and south ends of the station were changed to lighter shades and a similar change was made in the colored skylights.*

All of these changes were controlled by the management of the Indianapolis Union Railway Company, which at this point was being run primarily by representatives of the Pennsylvania Railroad, the Big Four, and the New York Central. Changes outside the station required the railroads to deal with city officials, the many shippers and freight handlers

(*Left*) Progress was brisk—and muddy—on both the track elevation and construction of the train shed. (Indiana Historical Society Bass Photo Co. Collection Neg. No. 68221F)

(*Below*) A carpenter on the train shed takes a brief break to pose proudly with his work-in-progress. (Indiana Historical Society Bass Photo Co. Collection Neg. No. 68491F)

in the city, property owners in the areas affected, and the general public. All of these groups had specific, and often conflicting, interests to press.

The first outside problem to be addressed was that of Pogue's Run, which flowed through the area and which had been a swampy barrier, an open sewer, an eyesore, and a flood threat since the old Union Depot was opened in 1853. In the summer of 1913 the city and the railway company signed an agreement regarding track elevations and the work to be done on Pogue's Run. After taking office in January 1914 Mayor Joseph E. Bell killed the plans of the previous administration. He said more practical plans would be drawn and there would be no delays in the track elevation and the Pogue's Run projects. But it was January 11, 1915, before a new agreement between the city and the Indianapolis Union Railway Company was signed.

The new plans, as well as the old, called for Pogue's Run to be routed underground through the downtown area to White River. At year's end, city civil engineer B. J. T. Jeup reported that the work on the stream was practically done and work on the track elevations had begun. "The Pogue's Run drain, costing with right-of-way practically $1 million," Jeup said, "is now completed with the exception of the construction of a few lateral drains and other appurtenances and the cleaning out of the drain."

Seventy-five percent of the cost of this work would be borne by the

July 30, 1918, saw the first train to load and leave from the newly elevated tracks at Union Station. The roof of the train shed was not completed until a couple of years later. (Indiana Historical Society Bass Photo Co. Collection)

(*Left*) So many trains steamed in and out of Union Station during the heyday of the railroads that some had to wait for others to move out before they could even enter the station. (Indiana Historical Society Bass Photo Co. Collection Neg. No. FOL 620)

(*Above*) Nearby trainyards were full of activity in the early 1920s. (Indiana Historical Society Bass Photo Co. Collection Neg. No. 88018F)

(*Right*) All twelve tracks are visible in this photo of the new train shed. Freight trains passed by on the tracks to the south of the train shed. (Indiana Historical Society Bass Photo Co. Collection Neg. No. 75296)

railroad companies and 25 percent by the city, Marion County, Woodruff Place, and the Indianapolis Traction and Terminal Company. The drain was planned to extend from White River and McCarty Street to New York Street, a distance of two and eleven-hundredths miles. The original plan provided two eight-by-sixteen-foot box culverts, eventually increased in size to eight-by-nineteen feet. The grades were made steeper and the capacity increased at critical points by at least one-third. The Pogue's Run culvert was clearly impressive. Eugene Brown, engineer on the Pogue's Run project, said the underground passage for the stream "was so big that when it was dedicated two processions of automobiles drove through it before they let water through." The completion of the work on Pogue's Run would enable the city and railroad companies to address the larger subject—elevation of the tracks.

In 1915 the Indianapolis Union Railway Company sold $4 million in bonds to fund a major part of the track elevation project and the construction of a new train shed at Union Station. In addition, it acquired some needed right-of-way and demolished buildings in anticipation of the track elevation work. War in Europe, however, caused additional delays. The State Council of National Defense passed a resolution recommending that track elevation work be discontinued during the war. Steel for track supports was slow in being delivered. Still, the city and the railroads were committed, and the work moved slowly toward completion.

On August 1, 1918, four permanent tracks with one permanent and one temporary passenger platform were put in service at Union Station on an elevated structure that had been erected in 1916 and 1917. Eventually, the new train shed was to have twelve permanent tracks, with three tracks for freight service south of the train sheds.

On October 1, 1918, the Indianapolis Light and Heat Company, under a contract dated July 1, 1918, began to furnish heat and light for the Union Station and the train shed. The station's old power plant was dismantled. By the end of 1919, the old train shed and the east and west end baggage buildings were demolished, and three permanent freight tracks, six permanent passenger tracks, and three permanent platforms were in use. Also, all trains were now operating on elevated tracks from West Street on the west side through Union Station and as far east as Delaware Street.

In its 1922 annual report, the Indianapolis Union Railway Company reported that the new train shed had been completed and that work on the passenger concourse underneath it was completed except for the installation of clocks, which was to be finished within sixty days. All track

The elevation of the tracks through the station and the completion of the new concourse underneath them made it possible for travelers to check tickets at the track entrance before going upstairs to their trains, thus eliminating the need to cross any tracks in order to board. (Indiana Historical Society Bass Photo Co. Collection Neg. No. 80338F)

This view of the head house in the early 1920s looks south toward the train information desk and the entrance to the concourse under the tracks. (Indiana Historical Society Bass Photo Co. Collection Neg. No. 330094)

In the new concourse, each gate served two tracks, and train information was posted for the appropriate track. Rookwood tiles used on the support columns added an elegant touch of class. (Indiana Historical Society Bass Photo Co. Collection Neg. No. 330101)

elevation work had been completed, except on tracks between East Street and Washington Street, which had been delayed by the construction of the East Washington Street Bridge. But now the city was agitating for elevation of the belt railroad tracks in other parts of the city, and by 1925 that work was under way.

The early years of the twentieth century were definitely the era of the railroad in Indianapolis, even through the years when the renovation was taking place. The number of trains arriving and departing from Union Station each year continued to increase. But in its 1924 annual report, when the railway company reported that "at the end of 1924, all construction work in connection with the elevation of Union tracks had been completed," it also reported the following:

> *Attention is drawn to the decrease in 1924 in the number of tickets sold at the Union Station ticket office. . . . The decrease in local ticket sales is probably due to the extensive use of privately owned automobiles and bus lines for interurban travelling. This decrease does not affect the income of the Indianapolis Union Railway Company, but [it] does affect the revenues of the tenant lines using these terminal facilities.*

A similar report was contained in the 1925 annual report. Now, with all the improvements in place for handling the demands of a railroad age at its height, that age had begun to decline.

When the tracks were elevated and the new train shed completed in 1922, twelve sets of tracks were available for use of passenger trains. (Indiana Historical Society Bass Photo Co. Collection Neg. No. 321567F)

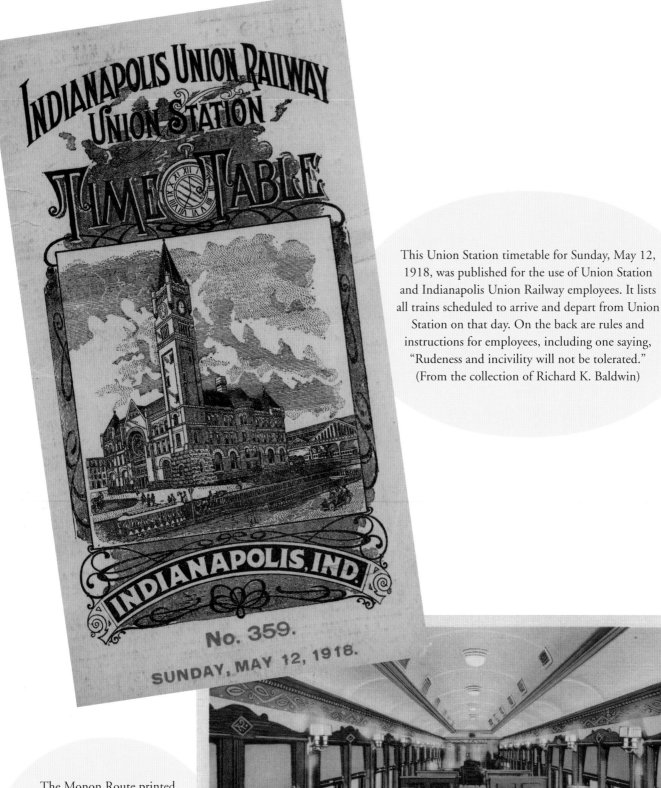

This Union Station timetable for Sunday, May 12, 1918, was published for the use of Union Station and Indianapolis Union Railway employees. It lists all trains scheduled to arrive and depart from Union Station on that day. On the back are rules and instructions for employees, including one saying, "Rudeness and incivility will not be tolerated." (From the collection of Richard K. Baldwin)

The Monon Route printed postcards in the 1930s to promote its elegant club-lounge cars, used on the *Hoosier*, which ran between Indianapolis and Chicago. (From the collection of Richard K. Baldwin)

CLUB-LOUNGE CARS — DESIGNED and BUILT BY MONON ROUTE

The station and train shed as they looked September 17, 1924. Freight trains were confined to the use of the tracks at the far left, running alongside the train shed. (Indiana Historical Society Bass Photo Co. Collection Neg. No. 88019F)

chapter 5
Train Travel Gets Competition

In the early years of the twentieth century, just about everyone who traveled any distance at all went by train. Indiana lay directly in the path of the expansion of American commerce and transportation. New rail lines continued to expand into all parts of the state even as small railroad companies were being swallowed up by large ones.

The first of the large rail networks to be fully formed in Indiana was the Pennsylvania system. Then came the Big Four Route, which later became part of the New York Central. By 1920 there were twenty-eight railroad companies operating in Indiana. Some were linked together as parts of the large systems. The twenty-eight companies owned a total of 7,812 miles of main and secondary track within the state.

By 1920, however, trains had serious competition. The first big rival of the steam railroad was the electric railroad, commonly called the interurban. The use of electric power for transportation began in cities with the streetcar companies, and by 1890 several Indiana cities, including Indianapolis, were replacing mule-drawn trolleys with electric streetcars. Electric streetcars connected Irvington with Meridian Street and went as far as Fairview Park (the present Butler University campus) by 1895.

The next step was to extend the tracks into the countryside and to connect with neighboring communities. The first interurban to enter Indianapolis was the Indianapolis, Greenwood, and Franklin, which arrived on January 1, 1900. By 1920 Indianapolis was the hub of the largest interurban network in the United States, which linked the capital city with almost every other major city in Indiana and which connected at three points with interurban systems in Ohio.

During World War II, Union Station was once again a popular gateway to Indianapolis, and parking space nearby was often at a premium. A new, longer marquee was built over the north entrance to the head house in 1941, shortly before this picture was taken. That was the last major improvement made in the station prior to its restoration in the 1980s. (Indiana Historical Society Bass Photo Co. Collection Neg. No. 267367F)

Servicing this network was the nation's largest interurban station, built in 1904 by the Indianapolis Traction and Terminal Company. It was located at Market and Illinois streets, just a few blocks north of Union Station, where the Adam's Mark Hotel stands today.

Steam railroads in Indiana began to lose some passenger business to the interurbans, particularly for trips of fifty miles or less. But the biggest threat to the steam, and the electric, railways proved to be the coming of the automobile and the motor bus.

In 1891 gasoline-powered cars were created independently by Charles Black in Indianapolis and John Lambert in Anderson, Indiana. Elwood Haynes began building cars in Kokomo in 1894. By the turn of the century, there were a number of automobiles in use in Indiana, chugging over dusty, rutted lanes and stopping to change tires scores of times on a one-hundred mile trip. Clearly, early automobile travel was not nearly as comfortable as traveling in the well-appointed passenger cars that came early in the century. Here one could eat endive salad and lamb chops on tables with silver and good china while watching the cows and silos of the Hoosier country go by. Flivvers were dirty, noisy, and scary—but not for long.

At the turn of the century, most of Indiana's roads were still unpaved, many impassable during wet weather. Toll roads constructed and operated for profit were the first paved roads. But as the popularity of the automobile grew, so did efforts to improve the roads.

In 1905 the Indiana General Assembly passed its first auto registration law, and in the first year 4,253 vehicles were licensed. The number rose rapidly, and in 1920 there were 333,067 registered vehicles in the state. The Indiana Highway Commission had been reorganized the previous year with instructions to lay out a system of state highways. Not only were significant numbers of Hoosiers owning and driving automobiles, but Indiana was also now a leader in the design and manufacture of automobiles.

According to the *Encyclopedia of Indianapolis*, the growing auto industry operated from more than fifty cities throughout the state. The automobiles manufactured in Indianapolis included the Marmon, the Cole, the Stutz, and the Duesenberg. Although the Indianapolis auto manufacturers gradually dropped by the wayside, nearly 100,000 motor vehicles a year rolled out of Indianapolis factories in 1920. Only a few years before (1909–1914), Indiana ranked third in the nation (behind Illinois and Pennsylvania) in the manufacture of railroad passenger, baggage, and freight cars.

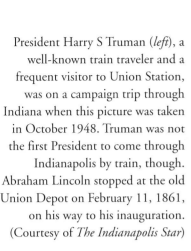

President Harry S Truman (*left*), a well-known train traveler and a frequent visitor to Union Station, was on a campaign trip through Indiana when this picture was taken in October 1948. Truman was not the first President to come through Indianapolis by train, though. Abraham Lincoln stopped at the old Union Depot on February 11, 1861, on his way to his inauguration. (Courtesy of *The Indianapolis Star*)

In its 1920 annual report, the Indianapolis Union Railway Company reported that it handled 64,343 trains at Union Station that year, an average of more than 176 trains a day every day of the year. The number declined slightly during the 1920s, but in 1930 the railroad still handled 58,976 trains at Union Station—a drop of only about fifteen trains a day.

Automobile travel became accessible to middle- and even working-class people, and the Model T and other family cars allowed freedom of movement, relative comfort, and efficient speed along increasingly improved roads. No longer did the traveler need to confine him or herself to the tracks along railway routes; by the twenties and thirties, wilderness areas became accessible and state and national park vacations available by auto. The first diners and drive-ins, such as White Castles and Steak 'n Shakes, opened around the country to serve the needs of motor travelers. No longer did families need to pay for dining-car meals or to travel on restricted schedules. Salesmen could set their own schedules to cities and small burgs. Freedom had come with four tires and a steering wheel.

The Great Depression helped accelerate the decline of train travel during the decade of the 1930s, as discretionary travel for many hard-pressed Americans fell off or ceased completely. The number of trains handled at Union Station dropped to 53,218 in 1931 and to 41,586 two years later. The numbers remained at about that level until World War II brought a revival of train travel. The war led to the rationing of tires and

The War Years

In a long, colorfully written story appearing May 12, 1943, The Indianapolis Times *captured life at Union Station during the war years. Following are some excerpts from that story:*

The station never closes, but if you should drop in between 2:30 and 4:00 A.M., you'd find the huge terminal at its emptiest, its silence punctuated by telegraphic tickings, the swish of the janitor's mop and the gentle snores of overnight bench-sleepers.

There's never an hour, however, when trains aren't roaring in overhead. In addition to troop trains, about 150 iron horses steam in and out of the station every 24 hours, most of them expresses and limiteds. The day of the local is over.

Although soldier travel constitutes the biggest transportation pick-up, station attendants are "pestered" most with the excessive civilian clientele. Civilians, not soldiers, usually are the chronic gripers, they say.

War has spawned an army of amateur travelers, many of whom have never been on a train before. Their foibles, say the station men, create a minor transportation bottleneck.

These novices frequently climb aboard wrong trains, exhibit a curious tendency to purchase wrong tickets, habitually lose their luggage, and ask superfluous questions like, "Do they serve cocktails aboard the *Jacksonian?*"

One ticket-agent commented: "A lot of these newcomers think they're starting on a great and glorious adventure when they buy a hundred-mile ticket. They want twice as much service as the average soldier or businessman, then complain because they don't get it fast enough."

One rule stands supreme among station employees. That's "servicemen first." If anyone is turned away from overcrowded trains, it's civilians. Soldiers, likewise, have priorities on Pullman and dining car accommodations.

Then, too, the United Service Organization (USO) has elaborate headquarters in the rear of the station, where servicemen are served free doughnuts and coffee, provided cots for overnight stop-overs, and entertained through various recreation facilities.

Many servicemen have benefited by the augmented staff of the Travelers Aid Society, [which] assisted 4,979 travelers in March of this year, as against 1,522 aided in March 1942. . . .

The station restaurant business furnishes a good criterion of the prosperous passenger traffic outlook. Irving Fendrich, the proprietor, says his business so far this year has increased 77 percent over last year's figure. He estimates that more than fifty thousand persons eat in the terminal lunchroom each month.

There's a gloomy side of the picture: Although responsibilities of red caps have multiplied, travelers aren't tipping as well as they used to. Red Cap Captain Robert Gilliam, a veteran of forty years at luggage toting, believes the shrinkage is due to a severe drop in "luxury travel." Most passengers these days aren't vacationing, he says, and none are on a world cruise—unless it happens to be an all-expenses-paid tour conducted by the armed forces.

gasoline, which curtailed travel by car. In addition, the movement of servicemen by train and the larger volume of mail generated by the war brought more business than Union Station had seen in years.

In 1940 the number of trains handled at Union Station totaled 42,477—only slightly more than seven years earlier. But in 1941 that number jumped to 45,668. The next year it exceeded 50,000, and in 1945 the number of trains using Union Station topped 60,000 for the first time since the 1920s. Some of the trains were so long they had to travel in sections, several minutes apart.

"Not since the lush era before buses and automobiles cut a sizable swath in rail passenger revenue," reported *The Indianapolis Times* on May 12, 1943, "have so many people stamped through the train gates to the tune of 'all-aboard.'

"Station veterans here agree that today's boom has never been surpassed. Troop movements, war workers and curtailed auto traffic are factors combining to cram the city's 'melting pot' at any time of day; but on weekends beginning at around 4:30 P.M. on Fridays the crowd reaches overflow proportions, milling impatiently around the time board and streaming out in long queues from half a dozen ticket windows."

Throughout the first half of the twentieth century, Union Station was a very busy place and an important institution in the lives of many Hoosiers. While the need to expand the facilities no longer existed after 1920 (except possibly during World War II), the station was redecorated in 1937, and a new marquee was built over the north entrance in 1941. In 1949 the Indianapolis Union Railway Company began replacing its steam locomotives with diesels (some passenger trains had begun using diesel locomotives as early as 1941), and in 1951 it mechanized the mail-handling facilities at Union Station. But little if anything new was to come after that. Following the end of the Korean War in the summer of 1953, the decline of passenger train travel was rapid and irreversible.

Love and War in the Grand Old Station

Following their marriage on Monday afternoon, January 3, 1944, Susanah Mayberry and her soldier husband, Frank, headed for Union Station to catch a train to Ithaca, New York, where she was to meet his family. The couple (right) was pursued from the wedding by a crowd of friends and relatives. This is her memory:

When we opened one of the big doors, we saw the huge station packed wall to wall with people. No gaiety here, families seeing their men off to war, spending every last moment they had together. Just a murmur of tired anxious voices. The depression was almost palpable. I think any one of the people there could have agreed exactly with the words that Frank spoke to my father when he asked for my hand. "My future is very uncertain."

Our friends and relatives were about to change the somber atmosphere with a roar of joy. We were still in the doorway. They opened both the big doors and made a "V" like migrating geese. By then we were kind of huddled in the middle as they charged into the mob, Moses parting the Red Sea. One of the men tenderly picked a sleeping infant from a bench and laid it in the lap of a surprised lady who was not its mother. Then he stood on the armrests and gave three piercing whistles with two fingers between his teeth. "We have a bride and groom here. Let's have three cheers," he shouted. He need not have shouted, as the crowd was temporarily stunned into silence by the whistles, but the cheers that followed nearly took off the high roof of the building.

I don't know whether there is a formula or an equation for spontaneous combustion, but I've seen it happen and I've heard it happen. Did eyes of strangers meet, or were there questioning, tentative grins on some faces? I don't know but everything exploded at once. Fatigue lifted, feet stopped hurting and hearts stopped hurting too. There was some sort of alchemy or infusion that happened to everyone there at the same time. It translated itself instantly into real gaiety and fun, and gaiety and fun were in short supply in January of 1944. . . .

The man who led the cheers yelled, "Let's sing. I'll take requests in order." "Mairzy Doats" yelled someone and then started the biggest, loudest sing-along in the history of the Western World. About three thousand voices. They were the songs we sang around the campfires of Leland, Michigan as the sun sank over the North Manitou and hits from the radio too: "Chattanooga Choo Choo," "Deep in the Heart of Texas," . . . "Don't Sit Under the Apple Tree," "Amapola," "Tangerine," . . . "You Are My Sunshine," and of course, "If You Knew Susie" and "Oh Susannah." Enough songs to sing for three hours with no repetitions.

Frank and I were separated in the mob and I wriggled myself to the outer edges of it. There I saw a curious sight; about six servicemen shoulder to shoulder and in a semi-circle facing outwards. I peeked over a shoulder and saw a very tired, very teary young woman nursing her baby. One of the young men said to me, "She couldn't get into the ladies room. It's probably closed for the duration. Damn the war."

After several centuries our train was announced. The crowd remembered us and started "Rock-A-Bye Baby." Everyone who could get onto the stairs leading to the platform did so. And, of course, they also went up the down staircase, not so much in a rush as a surge. An unstoppable rush of people and as many as could getting on the train. Our porter, may the gods smile on him, looked at us and said, "I'll get rid of 'em for you." He yelled "All aboard" about three times and they backed out reluctantly.

Going back to Indianapolis we had the same porter we'd had leaving three nights ago and he filled us in on what happened at the station after we'd left. He told us about his friend Harry, a porter in the next car. He went off-duty in Indianapolis. "Harry can't rest when there's singing and always has his harmonica in his pocket. He played for 'em. He say, 'I played 'On the Banks of the Wabash,' because they might get homesick, then 'Onward Christian Soldiers,' and that,' he say, 'really did take the roof off. He had to play that one twice. Then he played 'Abide With Me,' and, as the cleaning crew came in, 'Auld Lang Syne.' Harry, he thinks deep. He say, 'Why do there have to be war to make folks friendly?' He told 'em about a place to get coffee around the corner and he say, 'That station old and frumpy, but she kicked up her heels that night.'"

From *Of Love and Leland*
(Guild Press of Indiana, 1997)

Union Station is a part of many sweet and some not-so-sweet memories. Among those who share such recollections are these Australian war brides and their Hoosier husbands, pictured here as they were reunited at Union Station in March 1946, after a long separation following the end of World War II. (Courtesy of *The Indianapolis Star*)

A fifty-one-foot snow-white "Santa Colossal" towered over the main concourse at Union Station during the holiday season of 1949. It was part of the Indianapolis Industrial Exposition. Santa was made of Styrofoam plastic. His voice was a composite recording of Christmas greetings transcribed by orchestra leaders Spike Jones and Sammy Kaye and singers Eddie Arnold and Perry Como. Thousands of postcards bearing the giant's picture were passed out to visitors at the terminal. (Indiana Historical Society Bass Photo Co. Collection Neg. No. 109919)

A new cocktail lounge had just opened in Union Station when this photo was taken in January 1950. (Courtesy of *The Indianapolis Star*)

Crowds still jammed Union Station in the early 1950s when this photo was taken. Many travelers at the time were servicemen and women moving between duty assignments. Following the end of the Korean War, passenger train travel declined significantly. (Courtesy of *The Indianapolis Star*)

Trains had plenty of room in Union Station following the Korean War. By that time, commercial air travel was growing and construction of modern highways encouraged more people to take trips by automobile. (Indiana Historical Society Bass Photo Co. Collection Neg. No. 73201F)

The New York Central's *James Whitcomb Riley*, seen pulling into Union Station in this 1954 photograph, was the last "name" train to serve Indianapolis using a steam-powered locomotive. (Photo by Richard K. Baldwin)

THE NEW YORK CENTRAL SYSTEM

A Good Neighbor

INVITES YOU TO INSPECT

INDIANA'S FINEST STREAMLINER, THE

"James Whitcomb Riley"

AT UNION STATION

BETWEEN THE HOURS OF 12 NOON AND 10 P.M.

MONDAY, APRIL 21

*This train is a product of Beech Grove Shops,
one of the largest railroad shops in the world*

THE NEW YORK CENTRAL SYSTEM:

Maintains 236 miles of track in Marion County . . . a distance almost equal to that between Indianapolis and St. Louis.

Has 52 regularly-assigned switch engines, requiring five men to the crew for eight hours' work, serving 250 industries of Indianapolis.

Has 4,854 employes in Marion County, with an annual payroll of $8,513,718.82, who, with their dependents form a group of 19,416 customers for the merchants of I. N.

In 19__ . . . . $1.00.

. . . . N. Y. C.

. . . . in the
. . . . onage,

In Honor of a Great American

CENTENNIAL OF THE BELOVED HOOSIER POET 1849-1949

JAMES WHITCOMB RILEY

THE
James Whitcomb Riley
DE LUXE COACH STREAMLINER
Daily Between
CINCINNATI · INDIANAPOLIS · CHICAGO

NEW YORK CENTRAL SYSTEM

Dining Car Service

MARTINI COCKTAIL 40   SHERRY WINE 40   MANHATTAN COCKTAIL 40

Dinner
($1.00)

Wine Pickle

CHOICE OF: Chilled Celery   Ripe Olives

Hot Clam Bouillon   Gumbo Creole
V-8 Cocktail   Chilled Tomato Juice
CHOICE OF: Fresh Shrimp Cocktail

Fresh Lake Perch Saute, Meuniere
Salisbury Steak with Mushroom Sauce
Breaded Lamb Chops, Bordelaise
Roast Long Island Duckling, Apple Sauce
Grilled Small Sirloin Steak, Mushroom Sauce 1.75

French Fried Potatoes   Garden Vegetable   Parsley Potatoes

CHOICE OF: Assorted Rolls

Green Apple Pie
N.Y.C. French Vanilla Ice Cream
Rice Pudding with Sultanas
Camembert or Blue Cheese with Toasted Biscuits

Coffee

Tea

CORDIALS 60   Individual Milk

B. J. Bohlender, Manager Dining Service, New York

(*Above left*) In April 1940 the New York Central System invited the public to Union Station to see the *James Whitcomb Riley*, its prestigious train operating between Cincinnati and Chicago through Indianapolis.

(*Above right*) In the early '40s, as this menu shows, dinner in the diner on the *James Whitcomb Riley* cost one dollar—an incredible bargain by today's standards. For forty cents, the traveler could purchase a martini to go with the meal.

(*Left*) The New York Central System published a brochure promoting the "deluxe coach streamliner named in honor of the Distinguished Hoosier Poet." It was also filled with popular stanzas from famous Riley poems. (All from the collection of Richard K. Baldwin)

(*Above and left*) Well known to Hoosiers throughout the first half of the twentieth century was the Monon Line, an Indiana-based railroad running between Louisville and Chicago and Indianapolis and Chicago. The Monon was particularly popular with Indiana college students since it served such cities as Bloomington, Greencastle, Crawfordsville, and Lafayette. The old locomotive at left was photographed in 1959. (Photo by Richard K. Baldwin)

(*Right*) *Engine 999*, built in 1893 by Union State Express for the Chicago World's Fair, once set a passenger train speed record of 112.5 miles an hour. The engine was later restored at the Beech Grove, Indiana, railroad shops and is now on display at the Museum of Science and Industry in Chicago. This photo was taken at Union Station in June 1959. (Photo by Richard K. Baldwin)

(*Left*) A switch engine on the belt railroad that serves Indianapolis belched black smoke as it passed a crossing tower on the southeast side of the city. A railroad employee was stationed in the tower to throw signals and switches and pass on train orders. This photo was taken in 1953. (Photo by Richard K. Baldwin)

chapter 6
The Last Men to Serve

One can best understand the total and rapid decline of the passenger railroad train and its depot in Indianapolis by looking at the careers of two men who worked at Union Station from boom days to bad.

When Bernard C. "Ben" Wesselman and Floyd T. "Tom" Smith began working as mail handlers at Union Station shortly before the United States entered World War II, the old station was still a lively place. The cathedral-like head house was usually jammed with people, coming and going, night and day. Most were travelers on business trips or family vacations. Some were locals who dropped in for a haircut, a shoeshine, a newspaper, or a bite to eat. In the large mailroom under the east end of the train shed, where the two young men worked, bulging bags of mail were constantly being hauled in and out, coming from or going to the trains that rumbled overhead.

More than three hundred people were involved in processing mail at Union Station in the early months of 1941, and an equal number were employed elsewhere in the station. Union Station and about fourteen miles of track serving the station were owned by the Indianapolis Union Railway Company. On a 999-year lease dating back to 1882, the railroad also operated the belt railroad, with about sixty miles of track surrounding the city and serving major manufacturers and distributors.

Young and ambitious, Ben and Tom were excited about being a part of such a thriving enterprise. Who could have guessed in 1941 that they would in their careers witness the end of that enterprise and that Ben Wesselman would serve as the last station master and Tom Smith would serve as the last superintendent of the Indianapolis Union Railway Company to occupy an office in Union Station.

NIAGARA FALLS

YEAR-'ROUND Travel Guide

NEW YORK CENTRAL SYSTEM

YORK CENTRAL

SHORT VACATION TRIPS

Special Train Service
BETWEEN
=== INDIANAPOLIS ===
UNION STATION
AND THE
SPEEDWAY
DECORATION DAY
MAY 30, 1939
Running Time 12 Minutes

Commencing 6:45 A.M. and at 20 minute intervals until 8:00 A.M., thereafter at 15 minute intervals until the crowds have been handled to and from the Race.

20 Cents Each Direction

TRAINS WILL RECEIVE and DISCHARGE PASSENGERS IMMEDIATELY ADJACENT TO SPEEDWAY GATE!

New York Central System

(*Above*) "See how easy it is to go by train" was the message in brochures such as these from the New York Central System in the years following World War II. The brochures invariably contained lots of pictures and copy about popular tourist attractions, along with information on how to schedule your trip by train.

(*Left*) This little card promoted a very popular service that existed for many years—Race Day train transportation to and from the Indianapolis Motor Speedway. Notice the running time—twelve minutes! The service was discontinued in the 1960s. (All from the collection of Richard K. Baldwin)

Ben worked a couple of Christmas seasons in the Union Station mailroom before becoming a full-time employee in December 1940. In April 1943, in the middle of World War II, he was promoted to ticket seller and information clerk. In that position, he was considered by the government as too valuable to be called for military service—an indication of the importance of the railroads at that time. In April 1955 Ben was promoted to assistant baggage agent, and on January 1, 1956, he assumed the dual responsibilities of station master and baggage agent. Ten years later, he was given the added duties of ticket agent.

Tom began work as a mail handler in May 1941. The next year he became a locomotive fireman on the belt railroad, and in 1945 he was promoted to engineer. He became assistant trainmaster in 1956, trainmaster in 1958, and superintendent of the railway company in 1960. In that capacity, he was Ben's boss.

In 1960 the Indianapolis Union Railway Company had 640 employees, Tom said, and about half of them handled the mail that flowed through Union Station each day. At that time, most mail and parcel post was transported by rail. When the U.S. Postal Service stopped shipping

Floyd T. "Tom" Smith, at work in his office at Union Station, was the last superintendent of the Indianapolis Union Railway Company to occupy an office in the station.

Bernard C. "Ben" Wesselman (*far left*), the last person to serve as station manager at Union Station, talking with a group of conductors. It is believed that this picture was taken in October 1979, when the last passenger train stopped here before passenger service was discontinued. (Photo by Richard K. Baldwin)

much of the mail by train in 1971, choosing instead to use trucks and the airlines, the action had a devastating effect on employment at Union Station.

The rail passenger business had been declining since the end of the Korean War in 1953—actually to some extent since the end of World War II—as travel by automobile and commercial airline grew dramatically. According to records Ben kept, forty-three trains arrived and departed from Union Station each day in 1953—twenty trains of the Pennsylvania Railroad, twenty-one of the New York Central, and two of the Monon. By 1963 there were only nineteen trains arriving and departing from Union Station each day. The Pennsylvania had twelve, the New York Central seven. The Monon was no longer in operation.

By the late 1960s, Union Station—at least the head house—was no longer needed to serve the dwindling number of persons who still traveled by train. In fact, it had become a liability for the Pennsylvania and the New York Central lines, which jointly owned the Indianapolis Union Railway Company. "The railroads had refused to spend any money on maintenance of the station or the tracks," Tom said. "When I complained,

(*Above*) The *Southwind* pulls out of the station in 1965. By this time, some of the tracks had been removed because they were no longer needed. (Photos by Richard K. Baldwin)

(*Right*) When the *Southwind* stopped in Union Station in early 1959 en route to Florida, it was often so long it had to "double stop" in the station to pick up passengers, indicating quite a few people were still using passenger trains for some trips.

Although passenger service was dropping rapidly in the early 1970s, people were still riding the *Spirit of St. Louis* when this picture was taken in September 1971. (Courtesy of *The Indianapolis Star*)

they said their own roads were in worse shape than ours." For several years, Tom said, his office had been on the second floor of the head house, but the roof of the station got to leaking so badly that water came through two upper floors and eventually forced him to move to a ground-floor location under the train shed.

Not long afterward, in early 1968, the Pennsylvania and the New York Central merged, becoming the Penn Central. And the number of passenger trains serving Indianapolis each day dropped to fourteen. By 1971 the Penn Central was in deep financial trouble, and on May 1, 1971, the National Railroad Passenger Corporation formed Amtrak, a government subsidized corporation, to handle the nation's rail passenger business. The number of passenger trains serving Indianapolis was reduced to six a day.

That same year, Union Station's mailroom closed and the City of Indianapolis agreed to purchase the head house from the Indianapolis Union Railway Company to save the historic structure from demolition and to hold it until a private organization could raise money to buy and restore it.

On August 1, 1974, the few baggage and mail handlers still working at Union Station became employees of Amtrak. The number of trains serving Indianapolis dropped to four. A few months later the number fell to two, and the number of employees at the station was reduced to two janitors and five ticket sellers.

On March 29, 1976, all personnel left at the station were moved into the Penn Central Building at 31 East Georgia Street, and two days later Conrail was formed to replace the now-defunct Penn Central. Tom said he was named assistant terminal superintendent by Conrail, but he was given little work to do. He retired on March 4, 1977. Ben worked for Amtrak but was paid by Conrail. When in October 1979 the National Limited, running between New York and Kansas City, made its final stop in Indianapolis, the city was left without passenger service. On November 6, 1979, Conrail abolished the station-master position, and Ben retired.

For several years, attorneys continued to debate in court whether the Indianapolis Union Railway Company still existed, or whether it had been completely absorbed into Conrail's operations. But, for most persons, it no longer mattered.

Ben Wesselman and Tom Smith saw the station in good times and bad, and both shared many fond memories of their days at Union Station. Ben often recalled a visit by a regular train rider, then-President Harry Truman.

"His car was always on the head end of the train," Ben said, "and you know he liked to walk. When that train would stop in the depot, Truman would get off at Capitol Avenue and walk the train length all the way back to Meridian Street.

A Railway Express car and a mail storage car sit on a track at Union Station before the post office took the mail off the railroads. The back of the *Southwind* is visible on an adjacent track. (Photo by Richard K. Baldwin)

"I was always there to see if they needed anything, ice or anything, at the car. One time he said, 'I'm going to walk to the back end. Don't let the train leave without me.' And I said, 'Mister President, don't worry. If this train left without you, I wouldn't have a job.'"

Ben also fondly recalled a chance meeting with a young woman who stopped by his information desk one day in May 1943. That woman, the former Rosemary Selmier, became his wife on February 11, 1945. They had been married more than fifty-three years when Ben died on June 24, 1998.

Tom Smith was more concerned with railroad operations than with the station itself, but he said, "I retired twenty-three years ago, and I still dream about that crazy railroad."

When Ben and Tom retired, others, too, dreamed of the station's past grandeur and glory, and, through them, another era was about to begin for the venerable station.

Lingering snow kept the station and train shed covered in March 1965. (Photo by Richard K. Baldwin)

A political campaign train bearing local candidates made a stop on the near-Southside of Indianapolis in 1958. The Monon cars were borrowed by the Indianapolis Union Railway Company and used on the belt railroad. (Photo by Richard K. Baldwin)

Memories

My grandmother enrolled at Purdue University about 1912 or 1913, before very many women went to college. And, out of concern for her safety, her father would not let his daughter stay at school over the weekends. So she rode the train back and forth each week between Indianapolis and Lafayette. During that time, she bought a lot of train tickets and got very well acquainted with at least one ticket seller. And at the end of her first year at Purdue, she quit school and married the ticket seller.

— Mary Boggs

When I attended Indiana University in the early 1950s, Union Station was still a busy railroad station. Between forty and fifty trains passed through the station each day, picking up and dropping off hundreds, if not thousands, of travelers. And many of those passengers were students like me, traveling between Indiana colleges and universities and family homes in other states.

My family lived in New Jersey. When I bought my first train ticket in Union Station and boarded the eastbound Pennsylvania Railroad's *Jeffersonian* to go home for Christmas vacation, I was amazed to find what seemed like a whole trainload of IU students heading for Philadelphia, Newark, and New York City.

We were all traveling coach class—no Pullman berths or bedrooms. And the coaches, with their hard, straight seats, were old, dirty, full of squeaks and squeals, and often cold during winter weather. But most of the memories I have of those train trips are pleasant ones.

A party atmosphere usually prevailed. Some students played cards. Others sang, talked, or studied. The semester did not end before Christmas in those days; so, some worked on term papers due right after the holidays. And we all looked forward to the food vendors who passed through the cars when we stopped in Pittsburgh in the middle of the night.

The *Jeffersonian* was popular with students going East because it left Union Station about five o'clock in the evening and arrived at its destination the next morning. Those who could, and wanted to, slept much of the way.

— Jim Hetherington

Such wonderful memories—the 1920s—my childhood memories of the Union Station. My father, Charlie Miller, was a boilermaker for the Pennsylvania Railroad, so we got free passes and could travel a great deal. The excitement of checking to see if our train was on time, then the big, steaming monsters on track. . . . I was scared, but I knew soon I would be looking at lovely Indiana scenery zipping by at thirty-five or forty miles per hour.

Then there was the dining car with the white-coated waiters taking my order and so polite! Best of all was when we got to sleep in an upper berth. My brother and I would giggle and Mother would scold us to not wake other people. . . . The conductor would sing out the different cities, and when he said "Effingham" I knew we would be in St. Louis soon.

I am an old lady now, but I have a railroad lantern on my hearth. I have old silver, one serving; coffeepots, sugar bowls, creamers, [and] food covers, purchased . . . when [the] Pennsylvania Railroad and New York Central put the old dining-car service up for sale. Whenever I polish the old silver, my memories and tears come flooding back, I miss it all so much. . . .

—Annabel Miller Denny
From a letter dated March 3, 1986, written as a personal memory for the opening of the festival marketplace. The letter is one of several on display in the lower concourse at the station.

chapter 7
Death and New Life for the Old Station

In 1970, the Penn Central Railroad, which owned the Indianapolis Union Railway Company and, hence, Union Station, was bankrupt and trying to sell the station. It did not matter to the Penn Central whether a prospective buyer wanted to restore the facility or tear it down. At that moment, the City of Indianapolis began looking seriously at possible new uses for the station and, simultaneously, a group of railroad lovers, architects, history buffs, and students formed "The Committee to Save Union Station." The committee, headed by architect Dana Florestano, helped build public interest in the project.

There were those who wanted to demolish the head house and use the space for a parking lot. That idea was stymied by the cost of tearing down the station, estimated at $350,000. Many people had ideas for using the old station—a shopping mall, a museum, a school, a cultural arts center, a new transportation center, and an entertainment center for conventioneers. But no one stepped forward with an offer to buy the building.

Community leaders considered the station to be not only architecturally and historically worth saving, but also an asset to the redevelopment of that part of downtown, where the new Indiana Convention Center was to open in 1972. On August 3, 1971, then-Mayor Richard G. Lugar announced at a news conference in front of Union Station that the city would enter into negotiations to buy the head house and hold it until a private organization could raise money to restore the historic structure.

But rather than buying the station, the city wound up awarding its negotiating position to a private group called Union Station Associates. The group included the F. C. Tucker Company (a real estate company), Geupel-DeMars Corp. (a construction company), Baker, McHenry and

Richard G. Lugar, mayor of Indianapolis at the time, played a key role in the effort to save Union Station. On June 11, 1974, he applied good, old-fashioned elbow grease in cleaning the cornerstone at ceremonies marking the beginning of renovation work by Union Station Associates, a group of private investors who were not entirely successful, but who did keep the project alive. (Courtesy of *The Indianapolis Star*)

Welch (a mechanical contractor), and Browning, Day, Mullins and Dierdorf (an architectural firm). Robert D. Beckmann, Jr., an aide to Mayor Lugar, helped form the group and then left the mayor's office to join the Tucker firm and coordinate the station development.

Union Station Associates was awarded the right to purchase the head house in January 1973, and its nineteen individual and corporate members put up $500,000 to begin the repair work. The group bought the building from the Indianapolis Union Railway Company for $196,666. Its goal was to have the renovated facility in full operation by the end of 1974.

A plan to finance what was expected to be a million-dollar restoration was worked out, and preliminary agreements to lease about three-quarters of the space in the head house were signed. The group also had plans to add the train shed to the project later on. Then the oil crisis hit the nation, sending the rate of inflation, and construction costs, soaring. "Construction prices were going up at a rate of one percent a month," Beckmann said. "Our timing couldn't have been worse. It was just a disaster.

(*Left*) For a time in the 1970s, the station became a haven for street people. A station regular takes shelter from the chill of a November 1977 day and enjoys a discarded cigarette he found on the floor. (Courtesy of *The Indianapolis Star*)

By 1977 the Amtrak ticket office, located under the train shed in Union Station, was a quiet and lonely place. (Courtesy of *The Indianapolis Star*)

Unwilling to surrender the grand structure without a fight, a crowd returned to the dowdy old station on December 31, 1971, for a huge party to ring in the new year 1972 and raise money to help save the station from the wrecker's ball. (Courtesy of *The Indianapolis Star*)

"We'd get working drawings done, cost them out, and then get the bank to agree to all that. By the time we did that, the cost had gone up one or two percent so the drawings had to be redone or reduce the scope of the project."

By 1977 the group reluctantly came to the conclusion it had done its best without success. What the group thought it had proved, Beckmann said, was that the project needed some form of public subsidy if it was ever going to work.

In May 1978 the city's Capital Improvements Board concluded its own study by saying the most feasible use of the building—for rented office space—would still lose money. Renovation would cost $4 million to $6 million—too steep a price to pay for nostalgia. That's when the city began to look at the possible use of federal funds to save the station.

Indianapolis Congressman Andy Jacobs found himself very much in the middle of the controversy over the development of the old station. He had opposed the project, saying there "would be a few years of fad followed by a return to the handier watering holes of suburbia." But when the city found itself trying to bail out the unsuccessful investment and approached federal housing officials, Jacobs asked for and got a U.S. General Accounting Office appraisal of $350,000. In 1980, using community development block grants from the federal government, the city bought the head house from Union Station Associates for $474,000.

Beckmann said that although Union Station Associates lost close to $200,000 on the project, it succeeded in at least keeping Union Station standing. Eventually, through the continued interest and leadership of another mayor, William G. Hudnut III, the city received enough federal assistance to acquire the train shed, complete exterior work on both the head house and the train shed, and upgrade the Amtrak and Trailways bus facilities that were still in use on the south side of the station.

In the fall of 1980, rail passenger service returned to Indianapolis when Amtrak's "Hoosier State" train made its inaugural run between Indianapolis and Chicago. As part of the promotion of that service, there were some special train displays at Union Station. Along with these and the public interest came renewed hopes of turning Union Station into a transportation center once again.

Union Station had been added to the National Register of Historic Places in 1974, and city officials still considered the building a part of a strategy to revive the downtown. So they continued to look for the right use and the right people to make it happen. But it was two more years before Robert A. Borns, an Indianapolis real estate developer, came

During the years it housed a festival marketplace, Union Station was decorated for the holidays, and many special events were held there. (Photo by Darryl Jones)

forward with the proposal that breathed new life into Union Station. On September 16, 1982, *The Indianapolis Star* reported, "With only a handful of people looking on, the Metropolitan Development Commission yesterday accepted the bid by Indianapolis developer Robert A. Borns to turn Union Station into a dazzling new entertainment center and hotel."

"Borns' proposal and the commission's decision represent a dream coming true for Indianapolis," said Mayor William H. Hudnut at a press conference at Union Station following the commission meeting. The actual construction work on the state's largest redevelopment project began in December 1983 and continued to opening day.

Again, in 1986, Congressman Jacobs was approached by the city and asked to plead before the House Ways and Means Committee, of which he was a leading and influential member, that Union Station qualified for the highest possible transition tax relief under the historic restoration tax credit act. Still expressing his reservations because he believed the city should not be supporting private investors, Jacobs did so, hoping, he said, "to mitigate the damage."

On April 26, 1986, Union Station was reborn as a festival marketplace, where the attraction was a combination of food, shopping, and fun—and where the railroad remained a very obvious part of the history and decor. The day was marked by a big celebration. In the head house, the beautiful stained-glass windows, the archways, and the decorative plaster that gave the old station its charm had been painstakingly restored. In what was once part of the two-block-long train shed, a 276-room Holiday Inn displayed much of the station's superstructure, as well as thirteen Pullman cars now converted to twenty-six luxury suites. In what was now a food court, also formerly a part of the train shed, steel rails in the floor marked where the tracks had once been. Throughout the building, "ghost people" were nostalgic reminders of the railroad era and the reasons the station is so much a part of the community's heritage. "We're not creating something," said Borns prior to the opening of the festival marketplace. "What we are doing is polishing a diamond."

Borns and his wife, Sandra, were the geniuses behind this reincarnation of Union Station. They provided much of the creativity, enthusiasm, hard work, and money that brought the project to life. But saving Union Station had been at least a fifteen-year effort that would not have succeeded without the commitment of numerous individuals, and the heavy involvement of the local and federal governments.

Life-size "ghost people" were located around the festival marketplace to remind visitors of the scenes and the experiences that were regularly part of the station when it served train travelers. Sally Rowland of The Rowland Associates conceived and designed the ghosts. The Rowland Associates was responsible for most of the interior design work in the festival marketplace. Most of the ghosts now populate the Crowne Plaza Hotel and the new Grand Hall and Conference Center at Union Station. (Photo by Darryl Jones)

The food court, which had once been part of the train shed, was a popular place. In addition to the many food stands and restaurants, there was a stage where shows were presented several times a day. (Photo by Darryl Jones)

Robert and Sandra Borns—he in proper protective headgear—look over blueprints for the festival marketplace during the station's renovation. (Photo by Darryl Jones)

The old station—and the surrounding neighborhood—took on a new glow when the festival marketplace opened. And there was much disappointment when it eventually folded. (Photo by Darryl Jones)

(*Right*) When it was built in the remaining part of the train shed, the Holiday Inn at Union Station, now the Crowne Plaza Hotel, retained much of the superstructure from the old station, and it is still visible in the hotel today. In addition, the 276-room hotel still has twenty-six luxury suites in thirteen refurbished Pullman cars still on their original tracks (*below*). (Photos by Darryl Jones)

The exterior of the Crowne Plaza at Union Station still looks much like it did when the building was part of the train shed. (Photo by Darryl Jones)

Activity returned to the old head house in October 1999 when the Grand Hall and Conference Center opened under the management of the Crowne Plaza Hotel. Here the head house, now the Grand Hall, is set up for a banquet. (Photo by Darryl Jones)

A large reception area with a beautiful walnut Grand Bar adjoins the main dining room in the Grand Hall. (Photo by Darryl Jones)

chapter 8
Still at the Heart of Things

When the first railroad station in Indianapolis was built by the Madison and Indianapolis Rail Road in 1847, it was constructed on South Street a quarter of a mile from what was then the south edge of town. At first, there were complaints from the townspeople about the out-of-the-way location. But very quickly, the town went to the station. Businesses built up around it, creating for a time a commercial center there.

Subsequently, when the first Union Depot was built in 1853, it was also located on South Street, just a couple of blocks west of the Madison and Indianapolis station. And when the new Union Station was constructed in 1888, it was just north of the old one on virtually the same site. By this time the station was the center of a sizable commercial district that contained a large and vigorous wholesale trade, most of the city's principal hotels, and several small industrial enterprises. The railroads and Union Station formed the link with the outside world that attracted commerce and industry, and people, to Indianapolis.

Today, both Union Station and the surrounding Wholesale District are on the National Register of Historic Places. While they are no longer sustained by the railroads, they are still at the heart of activity in downtown Indianapolis. Just west of the old station, and linked by a walkway, is the Indianapolis Convention Center and RCA Dome, home of the Indianapolis Colts football team and center of the city's thriving meeting and convention business. In front of Holiday Inn's Crowne Plaza Hotel at Union Station is the Pan American Plaza, where many outdoor public events are staged. Just north of the station are the Omni Severin Hotel, the Canterbury, the Hyatt-Regency, the Westin Hotel, and the Embassy Suites. The major downtown hotels are still close by, just as they were a century ago. To the north and east of Union Station is Circle Centre, the community's downtown shopping mall, which has become immensely popular for its entertainment venues as well as its many shops, restaurants, and fine department stores. To the east is the new $183-million Conseco Fieldhouse, home of the Indiana Pacers basketball team.

The festival marketplace and the hotel at Union Station celebrated their tenth anniversary in 1996. The first decade was definitely an artistic success, but, for the festival marketplace, not entirely a financial success. The City of Indianapolis, which owns the station, was working hard to ensure that it would have an appropriate, and permanent, place in the life of the community. The restoration, involving both the festival marketplace and the adjoining hotel, is estimated to have cost more than $50 million.

The Crowne Plaza Hotel was a joint venture of Borns, developer of the festival marketplace, and James E. Dora, president of General Hotels Corporation, which operates six Holiday Inns and several other hotels in Indiana. The hotel at Union Station, with its railroad decor and its Pullman-car suites, has done well almost from the beginning.

In proposing the restoration and the new uses for Union Station, Borns said his "real goal was to save history for future generations." To make the project successful, he maintained a rapid-fire schedule of special events, many of them held in the large, open food court that filled the east end of the old train shed. In its first year, the festival marketplace attracted almost fifteen million persons. On a cash-flow basis, it was profitable during the first couple of years, according to Borns. But, by the end of its first decade, in spite of its lively and colorful beginning, the festival marketplace was failing.

The demands of operating the facility and managing the debt had caused Borns to turn the operation over to a Chicago-based firm, Moor & South Management Services, Inc., in February 1989. The debt was refinanced with a $23 million loan from Balcor Real Estate Finance of Chicago. In 1991 Balcor took ownership of the lease for the festival marketplace from Borns, and later that year it assigned its own property management division to run the facility.

In 1995, under liquidation orders from its parent company, American Express, Balcor sold the sixty-year lease at auction to USA Group, Inc., and wrote off more than $19 million in debt. USA Group, which administers student loans and provides information resources and consulting services to education, kept only the lease on the 852-space Union Station parking garage, which it needed for part of its work force that was moving downtown. The rest of the lease rights returned to the city administration.

So, the city went looking for another firm to buy or lease the old station and to breathe new life into the festival marketplace. The city administration believed that the debt-free status of the marketplace and the impending opening of Circle Centre, the city's long-awaited downtown mall, would enable a new operator to succeed at Union Station. Larry Gigerich, an aide to Mayor Stephen Goldsmith at the time, said, "Union Station is pretty much on the doorstep of the south end of the mall. It is very important that they work together to succeed."

But they didn't work together. Efforts to link the two with an enclosed passageway failed. And the success of Circle Centre did not rub off on the festival marketplace. Still, the city administration and others who believed in the old station's potential weren't ready to let go of the dream. In December 1995 the city put the station up for sale for $3.55 million, and

The station reopened as the Grand Hall and Conference Center on October 16, 1999, and the first event was the wedding reception of Bridget Ruth Durbin, of Indianapolis, and Timothy Parr, of Rowland Heights, California. Since renovation work in the station was going on right up to the time the party began, the bride and bridegroom came prepared with appropriately decorated construction hard hats. The second-level balcony was the perfect place from which to toss the bridal bouquet. (Photos by Cale and Whyte Studio)

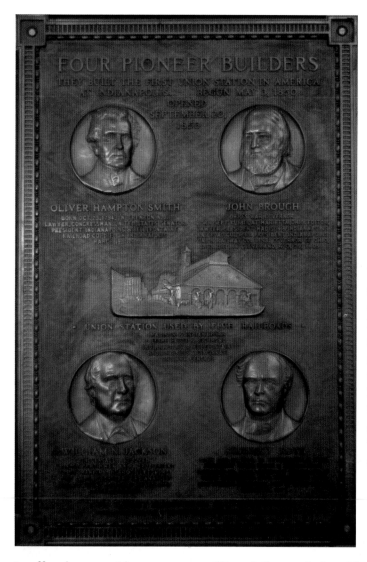

"They built the first Union Station in America at Indianapolis" states a bronze plaque honoring "Four Pioneer Builders": (*clockwise from upper left*) Oliver H. Smith, president of Indianapolis and Bellfountaine Railroad and a former U.S. senator from Indiana; John Brough, president of the Madison and Indianapolis Rail Road and later Civil War governor of Ohio; Chauncey Rose, president of the Terre Haute and Indianapolis Railroad and first president of the Indianapolis Union Railway Company; and William N. Jackson, secretary and treasurer of the Indianapolis Union Railway Company. The plaque was placed on the wall of the head house in 1914, and it is still there. (Photo by Darryl Jones)

it offered to provide up to one million dollars to help with repairs to the exterior of the building. By April 1996 the station was half empty, and there were no suitable buyers.

The city lowered its expectations and offered to negotiate with all interested parties. But, by November 1996, no suitable buyer or lessee was found, and Mayor Goldsmith announced that, to control costs, the marketplace, except for restaurants in the head house, would be closed following the NCAA basketball finals in March 1997. Within days of that announcement, officials of the Crowne Plaza Hotel at Union Station met with city officials to discuss the possibility of expanding into the retail portion of the station.

While the city continued to talk with any and all interested bidders, it frowned on most proposals because they relied too much on public subsidies. It favored the Crowne Plaza. A year passed. Some of the Crowne Plaza's ideas proved too costly for the hotel to pursue. Another idea—a parking garage in the station—was rejected by the city. Several more

(*Top*) The station today as seen from across the Pan American Plaza, and (*below*) a view of the plaza from an upper window of the head house. (Photos by Darryl Jones)

months passed. Ultimately, the city agreed to a five-year lease with the operators of the Crowne Plaza, who agreed to open a banquet hall and conference center in Union Station. The city also began making extensive repairs to the exterior and interior of the station. In April 1999 the Metropolitan Development Commission approved the new lease agreement. Six months later the Grand Hall and Conference Center at Crowne Plaza Hotel Union Station was opened, offering the sixth largest meeting facility in the Indianapolis area. There was new life in Union Station once again.

Those who nominated the old station for the National Register of Historic Places in 1974 said: "The Indianapolis Union Station is an outstanding architectural feature on the Indianapolis landscape that has survived intact the shift in focus of transportation, land use, and architecture. It recalls both in mass and detail (a time) when Indianapolis was a leading railroad center."

Sometimes the realization of a dream goes through several phases, and it is difficult to predict the final form it will take. But while the mix of businesses and activities in Union Station may continue to change, there is good reason to believe the historic structure will survive and prosper for years to come, for Union Station is still at the heart of an active and revitalized city.

Tracks 9 and 10 still serve passenger trains that stop in Indianapolis. The waiting area is located on the south side of the tracks behind the Crowne Plaza. In the summer of 2000, Indianapolis was served by two trains a day between Chicago and Jeffersonville, Indiana, and three trains a week between Chicago and Washington, D.C. (Photo by Darryl Jones)

Train and bus passengers now use this waiting room on the south side of Union Station at 350 South Illinois Street. Amtrak and Greyhound both have ticket offices here. Buses stop on the south side of the tracks, and trains come in overhead, much as they did in years past. The wooden benches are the same ones that had once been in the old Union Station waiting area. (Photo by Darryl Jones)

(*Above*) The Conference Center is located in the concourse under the train shed, where passengers once waited for their trains. The Rookwood tile pillars and the terrazzo floors, as well as the track gates, retain the flavor of the old station.

(*Left*) Muted lighting enhanced the architectural elegance of the main dining room when it was prepared for a special presentation. (Photos by Darryl Jones)

Acknowledgments

Much of the information contained in this book came from the newspapers that covered the events involving Union Station and the railroads over the last century and a half. The papers include *The Indianapolis Journal*, *The Indiana Sentinel*, *The Indianapolis Star*, *The Indianapolis Times*, *The Indianapolis News*, and *The Indianapolis Business Journal*. But I also made use of a number of reference books, including the *Encyclopedia of Indianapolis*, the *National Cyclopaedia of American Biography*, and city or state histories by W. R. Holloway, A. L. Logan, Max Hyman, Emma Thornbrough, Edward A. Leary, and Clifton J. Phillips.

In addition, I am deeply grateful to a number of individuals, who provided information, pictures, ideas, advice, and encouragement:

Erik C. A. Johnson, author of *Reflections on America's First Union Depot*, which I believe is the only other history of Indianapolis Union Station ever published.

Darryl Jones, who began photographing Union Station long before I began work on this book, and who provided almost all the color photographs in the book.

Richard K. Baldwin, also an excellent photographer and a railroad buff of the first order.

Howard Caldwell, an author and phenomenal researcher; Jerry Musich and Jerry Marlette, both railroad buffs and authors; Susan Sutton, coordinator of visual reference services for the Indiana Historical Society; David Lewis, reference librarian in the Indiana Division of the State Library; John Selch, newspaper librarian at the State Library; and senior photo librarian Charlesetta Means at *The Indianapolis Star*.

Also, Dr. Leslie H. Marietta, historian for the Edison-Ford Estates Museum in Fort Myers, Florida, who provided the information on Thomas Edison and who referred me to the Edison National Historic Site in West Orange, New Jersey, where I got the picture of Thomas Edison as a teenager.

Robert A. Borns and James E. Dora, without whom there would have been no restoration.

Betsy Wiersma, the first promotion manager for the festival marketplace at Union Station.

Ronald L. Haskell, Ricky Martin, and Travis Edenfield of the Union Station staff during the days of the festival marketplace.

Fountain waters dance in the breeze on the Pan American Plaza . . .

Sally Rowland, who is responsible for the "ghost people" and much of the rest of the interior design of the renovated station.

Evert Hauser, who represented the city's interests at Union Station; Reid Williamson of the Historic Landmarks Foundation of Indiana; and Dr. James A. Glass, director of graduate programs in historic preservation at Ball State University.

Bernard C. Wesselman, the last station master, and Floyd T. Smith, the last superintendent of the Indianapolis Union Railway Company based in Union Station; and several helpful people at the Indianapolis-Marion County Public Library.

I reserve my biggest thank you, however, for Bob McElwee, who conceived the idea for the book and encouraged me to write it, and my publisher, Nancy Baxter, of Guild Press of Indiana, who helped me in many ways. Also, Megan McKee, who edited my manuscript; editor-designer Sheila Samson of Guild Press; and Dick Listenberger, of Listenberger Design Associates, for the dust jacket.

Finally, Gene King, construction manager and coordinator of the most recent renovation of Union Station. When conflicting figures appeared for the ceiling height of the head house, Gene was willing to measure it and ensure accurate figures for the book.

. . . as strollers enjoy a sunny Sunday afternoon. (Panoramic photos by Darryl Jones)

The following item appeared in a special issue of American Heritage *magazine entitled "Overrated Underrated" (May-June 2000). The article was written by John H. White, professor of history at Miami University, Oxford, Ohio, and a former curator of transportation at the National Museum of American History.*

Most Underrated Railroad Station
THE INDIANAPOLIS UNION STATION OF 1853

This is rarely mentioned in historical texts, yet it appears to have been the first to collect all the major rail lines entering a city and put them in one building. The building was hardly a marble palace, nor did it likely spend much in the way of gilt ornamentation. It [the original Union Depot] was just a great barn, 425 feet long by 200 feet wide, a cheap commercial structure built for a purpose rather than a look. Here, passengers could change trains for destinations throughout the area just by walking between platforms. Platform 1 might be limited to trains for Cincinnati, Platform 2 for Madison and Louisville, and so on. By 1870, it was serving eleven railroads and handling seventy-six trains a day.

A few other cities, such as Chattanooga and Cleveland, followed Indianapolis in just a few years. But other major cities punished rail travelers with the old inefficient multiple-station system.

Index